WHY CAN'T I SPEAK

by

Barbara Naughton

authorHOUSE®

AuthorHouse™ UK Ltd.
500 Avebury Boulevard
Central Milton Keynes, MK9 2BE
www.authorhouse.co.uk
Phone: 08001974150

First published by AuthorHouse 10/2/2007

ISBN: 978-1-4343-1643-1 (sc)

D177,492
£14.99

364/1536

*Printed in the United States of America
Bloomington, Indiana*

This book is printed on acid-free paper.

ACKNOWLEDGEMENTS

I would like to thank the Galway Rape Crisis Centre for their Support during my father's Trial. I would like to thank my counsellor Susanne for helping me during the trial and showing me a light at the end of the tunnel. I would like to thank Jim Mitchell (R.I.P) for his assistance during my father's trial. I would like to thank Alan Carroll for his assistance and advice after my father's trial. I would like to thank Chris Giblin who was very supportive and helpful after the trial. I would like to thank Peter McGarry, Solicitor, for his legal advice and friendship. I would like to thank Kate Mulkerins for her constant support. I would like to thank Caoimhin O' Caolain, TD, for his efforts on my behalf. I would like to thank Katherine Dewar, a beautiful human being. (shamanic healer and Soul retriever) from Boston for her inspiration, guidance and healing. Special Thanks to my pals in New York, Mohammed and Hertzel. Finally, I would like to thank my Publishers, Author house, for making the Publication of my Book an interesting experience. Thanks to Judy Broadbent, my Publicist. I would like to dedicate this Book to the Galway Rape Crisis Centre and to all victims of child sexual Abuse. I hope that this Book will make it easier for other victims to come forward and tell their stories.

INTRODUCTION

Early in April 2002, Patrick Naughton appeared in the Central Criminal Court, Dublin, charged with raping his young daughter behind the closed doors of their country home in county Galway. Mr. Naughton was given an 11-year sentence by Mr Justice Philip O' Sullivan. The length of sentence came as a great relief to his daughter. Not only did it vindicate her actions in bringing her father to court, it also removed for a long time the threat he made that he would come after her again.

In court, it emerged that the rapes, often accompanied with violence, sexual abuse and psychological abuse had occurred repeatedly over a period of six years, from 1987 – when Barbara was only 8 years old – to 1993, and once again in June 1997.

This final rape convinced Barbara Naughton to report her father to the authorities. As he was raping and choking her, Barbara vowed to herself that if she survived, she would come forward and tell her story.

When she did, the case split her family. Initially, her brothers sided with her father. Ann Naughton, Patrick Naughton's sister, also took the side of the her brother and went to extraordinary lengths to try and influence the outcome of the trial.

Many shocking details were revealed in Court:

How Patrick Naughton had raped the small girl almost weekly. How he had threatened to kill her by throwing her in a bog with a stone around her neck. How he found out that she dreamed of becoming a model and a singer and broke her nose. How he had almost choked her to death on the night of June 19, 1997.

Patrick Naughton told the court that all the allegations were "a pack of lies". However, the jury of five women and seven men did not agree. After four-and-a-half hours of deliberations spread over two days, they returned a unanimous verdict of "guilty" and Patrick Naughton was given an 11 year sentence by Justice Philip O' Sullivan.

But that was not the end of the story. At the sentence hearing, Justice O' Sullivan, revealed that he had been approached by the office of a Minister of State, Deputy Bobby Molloy, in relation to the case. A Department of Justice official had put a call through to the judge regarding the case. Later, a second caller had rung to ask if the judge had received a communication from the convicted man's sister, Ann Naughton. The judge also told of having received two envelopes addressed to him that he had not opened. In publicly criticising what he called this "totally improper approach" the judge set in motion a media storm. Ministers – including John O' Donoghue (who at the time was the Minister for Justice) – jumped to Deputy Molloy's defence. Barbara Naughton called on Deputy Molloy to resign. The contemporary Taoiseach, Bertie Ahern and Deputy Molloy's political colleague Mary Harney refused to see it as a resigning matter. A series of statements, by government TDs, publicized a system whereby politicians considered nothing unusual or unethical in such contacts.

It didn't seem to trouble any of these politicians that as Barbara Naughton lay awake at night, praying that justice would be done, Deputy Molloy was passing letters that insinuated that Barbara Naughton was a liar. Or that Deputy Molloy, knowing that Patrick Naughton had been found guilty of rape, assault and buggery, and that he had threatened to kill Barbara for speaking out, nonetheless passed on a query asking for an early release. To them, it was all just normal constituency business.

As the media exerted pressure and more details of the case entered into the public arena, Deputy Molloy finally consented to do the honourable thing and resign. In his resignation speech, Deputy Molloy apologized to the public and referred to Barbara in his apology. He said that he was deeply sorry that his actions "may have compounded her pain."

Barbara Naughton's nightmare did not end the day the abuse stopped, or the day her father was jailed. She has suffered serious stomach disorder, teeth problems from grinding them in her sleep, bulimia, asthma, panic attacks and has attempted suicide due to her experiences and neglect.

Barbara is an articulate young woman of outstanding courage and seems to succeed in any field she now applies herself to. She has obtained qualifications in all courses she has attended and is currently studying Law. Barbara is currently working on a screenplay. As a child, she enjoyed singing. However, due to her painful childhood experiences, this talent was suppressed. Barbara, thankfully, has renewed her love affair with music and is currently writing her own songs. Recently, Barbara attended a Shamanic Spiritual Healer in the United States in an effort to retrieve her lost childhood. She has also attended Past-Life-Regression and hypnotism sessions in Ireland. She feels that she has now retrieved her soul and is now in a position to move forward. She has managed to surmount her illnesses and very understandable anxiety in order to come forward and speak her truth. It is Barbara's hope that this book will inspire and encourage all those who read it to understand that it is not the victim who should be ashamed, but the abuser.

This is Barbara's story in her own words.

PROLOGUE

CONNEMARA CO. GALWAY

My name is Barbara Naughton. I was born and raised in Connemara, Co. Galway. My father, Patrick Naughton, married my mother Maureen Folan. My father came from a large family and had 11 siblings. My mother also came from a large family. When my father and mother married they eventually settled in Kinnvarra, Camus, a small rural village in the West of Galway. The village was situated in a Gaeltacht (an Irish Speaking Region), and I, like my two brothers, Niall and Tony and my two sisters Aoife and Grainne, was brought up speaking Irish as my first language. The house in which we lived was situated in quite a remote area. My father never worked much in his life, other than tinkering about with cars or applying his handyman skills to "upgrading" our home. My mother worked whenever the opportunity arose and generally took care of students attending Irish Summer Schools during the Summer. When I look back at my childhood the first memory that springs to mind is my first day in National School.

NATIONAL SCHOOL

When the preordained morning arrived, I hurriedly dressed and joined my mother and father and siblings in our kitchen for breakfast. After breakfast, I entered our sitting room where my father was cleaning out the ashes from the grate as he always did. I asked him if he enjoyed school when he was a child. He told me that he didn't enjoy school and that he hated his teachers who used to beat him for nothing. I looked at him with a puzzled expression on my face. He then told me that I would be in school til 3 o'clock, but that I wasn't to worry as the teachers would probably be soft on me as it was my first day. I turned and left my father and approached my mother who was preparing my lunch and arranging my little school satchel. I asked my mother why the teachers in my father's school beat him. She told me not to listen to what my father said and to grab my coat as we were about to leave. As my mother and I walked out our hall door, my father appeared from the sitting room and asked my mother "Don't you think that she is a little young to be starting school." My mother turned and replied "Well that's the age I see all the children from the neighbourhood starting school." My mother turned towards me and we walked down the hill towards the National School.

After a ten minute walk, we finally arrived outside the gates of the National School. I was nervous and when my mother told me to run into the school and join the other children, I looked up at her, crying at this stage, and told her that I didn't want to leave her. She looked down at me with sympathy in her eyes and told me that I would make lots of new friends and that she would be returning to collect me in a couple of hours. I was not convinced and pleaded with her to take me home with her. Suddenly, a tall woman approached holding a young girl's hand and told me that she would bring me into the school. The young girl smiled at me, held my hand and led me into the school grounds. As I turned, I spotted my mother turning towards home, her brown bucket in her hand. She was obviously heading to the well to get water before going home.

When I entered the school, I was amazed at how large the building was. There were other children running around everywhere. The tall woman lead me into a room and told me that this was my classroom. I looked around. There were 20 other children seated in the room. Seconds later, another tall woman arrived. She introduced herself as Ms Carter and told us that she was our teacher. She appeared very friendly and I immediately felt at ease. My first day in National School was a delight. Ms Carter allowed all of us to draw pictures and play with our teddies until our parents collected us later that day.

My First Communion

A couple of years passed and it wasn't long before I was preparing for my Holy Communion. In School, Ms Carter, arranged music classes for us so we could sing at our Holy Communion. I had at this stage become a regular member of the class choir and we regularly performed in the local church in Camus. I loved singing and I loved performing. At this stage of my life, I had resolved to become a famous Country Singer, like the American Country And Western singers I watched on television at home.

One afternoon, after finishing singing lessons, I came home from school with my brother to find my parents out. I remembered that they had told us earlier that morning that they might not be home when we returned from school. Unusually, we couldn't find the front door key under the mat on our doorstep to get in. We checked under the geranium pot where they also placed the keys, but found nothing. My brother suggested that we should stay with our granny next door until our parents returned. My granny was sitting beside the window knitting when my brother and I walked in. I asked her what she was knitting? She told me that she was knitting a pair of gloves. I told her that I was learning how to knit in school. I told her that I only worked with two needles. She used three needles. She explained that she had learned how to use three needles in school and that it was sometimes easier to use three depending on what type of knit-work you were doing. She told us that she found it easier using three needles when knitting a jumper. I told her I was knitting a scarf as it was the easiest item for me to start on. She asked me if I was looking forward to my Holy Communion that was fast approaching. I told her that I was looking forward to wearing the beautiful white dress and white gloves that my mother had bought. Our parents came home from town shortly afterwards and my brother and I helped carry in the weekly shopping, as we always did. We checked every bag for sweets, but sadly found nothing.

Later that night I woke from my sleep and heard shouting and crying. I slept in the room next door to my parents bedroom and from there I overheard my father shouting. By the sound of his voice, I knew he had drink taken. Suddenly, everything went quiet. I was frightened and couldn't sleep. I was disturbed by my father's loud voice and then, the eerie silence. My brothers slept in the bunk beds across from me. I looked across to see if they were awake. I didn't see them move. Perhaps they were awake and didn't want to imagine that they had heard all that shouting. I looked again at them and wondered.

The following morning, I heard my father rushing around the house whistling. What had I learnt about my father whenever he whistled? He was either up to something or had already done something wrong. As I lay in bed, an uncomfortable feeling gripped my chest as I listened to him. I jumped out of bed and dressed quickly. I headed towards the kitchen and spotted my father carrying a bag of ice towards my parents bedroom, a look of concern on his face. My father entered the bedroom and closed the door behind him. I followed him and knocked on the bedroom door and asked if I could come in. My younger brother Niall passed in the hallway and said, "Ssssh! Leave it. Don't go in." I opened the bedroom door and spotted my mother on the bed holding an ice pack to her arm. I asked my mother what had happened? She replied that she had fallen and injured her arm. I knew she was lying and that my father had struck her. I gave my father a look of disgust. If only I was older, I would have attacked him immediately. I looked at my mother's arm again and a feeling of rage engulfed me. My father told me in no uncertain terms to leave the room immediately.

Later that afternoon, when my father went out, I asked my mother what had actually happened. She claimed that she had fallen off the chair whilst reaching for something on top of the cupboard. I knew my mother was lying, but at that stage of my life had no understanding of adult relationships. I didn't press her on the issue. For days afterwards, the atmosphere in the house was unbearable. Sometimes, my parents would pass each other in the house without speaking. My father moped around the house cursing all the time, giving out about silly little things. For example, a piece of paper on the floor. If the car didn't start, he would complain to whichever one of us was in the car at the time. I was unable to understand the behaviour of this adult, whose moods changed in a matter of seconds. I began to wish that we could just move away with mam. Other times, I thought I would be happier if my mother got the tongs or a hammer and hit my father over the head and knocked him out. As weeks passed, the atmosphere in the house gradually improved and the day before my Holy Communion, I sat on my bed and looked at the cards that I had received. There were cards from all my relatives, but the most beautiful one of all was from mam and dad. I opened it and read the verse written on the inside of it

'May the Lord Jesus Bless and protect you today and all the days of your life'

Underneath mam had written, 'to Barbara with lots of love, from mam and dad'. I counted the kisses and there were seven altogether, one for every year of my life. When I had finished reading all the cards, I picked out a heart-shaped rosary box that my grandmother had given me for my Holy Communion, opened it and lifted the crystal beads up by their silver cross. They glittered like the colours of a rainbow in the sun. I twirled the cross and the colours changed and danced about the ceiling and walls. I put out my hand and slowly lowered the beads onto my palms. To me they resembled a cluster of diamonds winking in the sun. Mam said that I could only use the beads for feast days as they were too delicate for everyday praying. I carefully placed them back into their box and tucked them into the corner of the shoebox.

Later that evening, I asked my mother where she had bought the dress. She told me that a family member had given it to her. I went to sleep that night dreaming of my special day to come. The following morning, when I woke, I got dressed in my Communion clothes. After breakfast, my father asked me to follow him outside. As we walked, my father held my hand and led me to the front door of our house. My father told me to close my eyes which I did. When I opened my eyes, I saw our dark blue car, looking as good as new, the centre of the wheels shining. When we returned into the house, my father told me that he wouldn't be standing at the altar with me while I was being confirmed. Immediately, I looked in my mother's direction and asked her what my father meant. My mother told me that my father disliked the church. When my mother tackled my father on the issue, he merely replied that he had no intention of entering the church or standing beside me at the altar as I was being confirmed. He also informed us that he had not stood at the altar when my eldest brother Tony had been confirmed. When I told my mother that our teacher had insisted that both parents should stand with their children as they were being confirmed, my father merely left the house and told us that he would wait for us in the car. This was the first time in my life that I felt my father had little affection for me or my siblings. His behaviour was impossible for a seven year old to understand.

Later that morning, my aunt called round to join us for the special day. When we arrived outside the church my father told us all that he would wait in the car until the ceremony was over. When my mother, aunt and I entered the church, we noticed that all the other children and parents were dressed nicely and many of the mothers were wearing nice hats. We continued up the aisle of the church and took our seats directly in front of the altar. As the mass continued, one of my relatives turned to me and told me that my school gang was heading towards the altar. I immediately followed my classmates towards the altar. As my classmates and I were confirmed, all the relevant parents were present other than my father, unless one of my classmates parents were dead. I felt disappointed that my father didn't stand with me on this special occasion like all the other parents had done. When the mass was finished, I received several cards. As I stood on the altar with my classmates, my mother's sister took several photographs.

Outside the church, many more photographs were taken. My father joined us and consented to be in some of them. When I had finished congratulating some of my friends from school, my mother and I walked towards our car. When we arrived back at the car, my father was talking to some of his friends. He invited them to our home for drinks later that evening. My father's friend had two daughters making their Communion on that day with me. When they arrived at our home that evening, they took several photos of their daughters and me. After having something to eat, we all headed off to the local pub. In the pub, I had a great time with the girls. We played with machines in the pub as our parents sat in a corner drinking and chatting. I enjoyed the time with my school friends. We were trying to learn how to play pool against my brothers. I told the girls proudly that from that day on we would be able to receive communion every week.

The following February, my youngest sister Aoife was born. Aoife was one of those children who wanted to be heard. When my mother returned from hospital with the new baby, I barely recognised her as she had lost so much weight. When I asked my mother where the new baby came from, my grandmother intervened and told me that my mother had bought the baby from the shop at the bottom of our hill. But somehow, I was not convinced as I had never seen a baby on any of the shelves in the shop. Mam stood there and laughed. My mother then handed me my little sister to hold. Moments later, my brother Niall rushed into the house and asked my mother whether the baby was a boy or a girl. When my mother told Niall that it was a girl, a look of disappointment crossed Niall's eyes. I laughed at Niall and jokingly told him that there were more girls in the house now and that we were stronger than him and he would not be able to bully us anymore. He told mam that she should have another boy and send the baby girl away as girls were troublemakers. As he left the room, he said "mam can't you see the troublemaker smiling." I merely laughed and kept on smiling. The anger on his face increased.

As Winter ended, and Spring arrived, my siblings and I were looking forward to the good weather as it rained incessantly in Galway. At that time, back in the mid 1980's, when I was a child, people in my community visited each other on a daily basis. There seemed to be a great atmosphere in our locality and always something exciting happening in the village. Our neighbours would always throw a nice party whenever a child had a birthday. Our relatives visited regularly, including my great-granny who lived across the road from our home. When our parents journeyed to Spiddal or Galway, my father's family across the road generally baby-sat us. I was very close to Ellen, my father's youngest sister. I used to enjoy her company a lot. She used to tell me wonderful stories and act them out. That always made them more interesting to listen to. I also loved my granny very much and would often go 'over the wall' to tell Granny the kind of fun I was having in school. I really liked her, my father's mother. Whenever she was around, I felt very happy. On one occasion, during that Winter, I recall my granny calling my brothers and I into her house. Initially, we thought we had done something wrong. However, when we entered the house, our granny gave us all a bag of Tayto crisps. I used to love looking at the image of the Tayto man on the bags and would constantly torment my mother with his image. Whenever she would tear a bag, I would tell her that she was hurting the Tayto man.

During that Spring, my mother was obliged to stay in Galway hospital for several nights. At home, my father seemed to be spending more and more time in the pubs in my mother's absence. One night, after coming home from the pub, I recall my father trying to climb onto one of the bunk beds in our house. As he tried to climb onto the bunk bed, he slipped and fell. He lay on the ground motionless. I approached him and started to shake him. Slowly he came to. He cuddled me and then headed towards his own bedroom. As a child of eight, I lay on my bed, feeling sorry for my father. I innocently believed he missed my mother. Sadly, I was shortly to realise that this was not the case.

FIRST EXPERIENCE
OF ABUSE

One Sunday morning in May 1987, I had to stay back from mass. It was a few months before my 9th birthday. Mam told me to tidy my room while they were at mass. I grabbed the skipping rope and skipped down to my room. I rushed around putting my clothes anywhere they could fit, even under my bed. In a matter of minutes my room was as tidy as a doll's house. I tidied the toys away and opened the zip on the big Teddy Bear's pocket and stuff ed it with the rest of the clothes that were lying around, so the room would look clean when mam returned. I wrapped Vefin, my favourite Teddy Bear in his blanket and tucked him into the corner of my wardrobe to hide him from my mother, because every time she spring-cleaned the room she went on about 'that scruff y old teddy' and had threatened to throw him out. I knew he was safe in there, hidden from her. But I was not safe. That morning I was sexually abused for the first time. I have little recollection of this initial experience. However, as these occasions of abuse reoccurred, I began to feel like I was being punished for some wrongdoing. On these occasions, I felt as if something was overwhelming me as I was being raped by my own father. Words couldn't describe how broken I felt. It was as if my heart had physically been ripped out of me. As he was a heavyset man, when he lay on top of me there was so much weight on me. I do know that I couldn't move or breathe. I didn't understand what was being done to me. This was not right, I kept saying to myself. I switched off from what was going on. I didn't want to look at him. It was a horrible feeling and the excruciating pain was hard to explain. I started screaming and crying out loud, asking him to leave me alone. I tried to push him away but I wasn't strong enough. He wouldn't listen. He didn't care. He showed no pity for me when the tears came from my eyes. He didn't stop. He told me to keep quiet. I felt numb and speechless afterwards. The frozen feeling inside wouldn't allow me to peak afterwards. I wanted to run out of the house and scream. My head felt strange. My father's voice was like an echo talking away; trying to bring me back to reality and promising that he wouldn't hurt me again. He started talking about the facts of life; as if we had all day to talk before the rest of the family arrived home. He went on and on for ages about what people put up with in their own homes, things that words couldn't describe. My father told me that children throughout Ireland had to deal with much worse. He said some children were beaten on a regular basis. He told me what he had done was normal and that I was not to tell anyone.

Mam returned home later that afternoon and my older brother came back from his friend's house. There I was, still a little numb, my father sitting across from me giving me the eye, trying to ensure that I would have a bright face on for my mother. My father gave me several warnings to keep up an appearance when my mother returned. I was tired of him calling me aside, telling me that I looked miserable. He told me to put a 'happy face' on for my mother.

Two weeks later the abuse reoccurred, in my bedroom this time. The rest of my family were out of the house. My two brothers were outside playing soccer with my aunt. I wasn't allowed to go out with them. I had an uncomfortable inner feeling that something was about to happen, the way some people can sense danger when it's on the way. I tried to join my siblings in the garden, but my father told me to remain in the house. He kept me inside, undressed me and forced himself on me again. I was extremely upset and powerless. My father helped me put my clothes on. I was numb and speechless. My father said: "Jesus Christ Almighty, you'd think you were going to have a heart attack or something, you look awful pale." He told me to clear my eyes, as there were tears flowing from them. It was a lovely sunny day. However, I was clouded inside, in no state to be playing soccer after what my father had done. Suddenly, I began to tune into the noises outside, my brothers laughter. I was in the sitting room taking deep breaths, when my elder brother entered the house and asked me if I would like to join them. There was no way that I could have any privacy to talk to my brother about the reason that I couldn't join them. My father was holding up the wall with his ear to the door. He always listened every time I tried to talk to any member of my family. I used to hear him pushing in the door slowly. From that day on, my father made every effort to restrict my freedom and ensure he was aware of my comings and goings.

The following morning, I sat at our kitchen table eating breakfast. I had little interest in my food. I began to feel uncomfortable at that stage with everything. A feeling of disgust and self-hatred began to pervade my mind. I was preparing for school and thinking about everything that my father was going on about, things that I didn't need to learn yet as I was only 8 years of age. My head was full with it. Later that afternoon as I sat on the steps outside the school, I wondered what was the point of it all. Why play football, basketball, do anything for that matter? I wondered why my father was hurting me.

Days later, my father described things that women had to put up with and how they suffered. I had to listen to him, sitting with a glass of homemade poitin in his hand. The more he drank the worse he got. He insisted on showing me a pornographic video. I wouldn't look at it. I turned my face away. He told me that I had to watch it as I needed to learn the facts of life. On watching the film, my father commented on how men would tear the clothes off a woman with a knife if she refused to have sex with him. He told me that no man was sane out there. My father told me that men only abused women and used them like rubber dolls. He also named a few men from our locality who were cheating on their wives. He kept replaying the film even though he knew I didn't want to watch it and that it made me sick. After watching that video, he tried to abuse me again. I got up and rushed to my bedroom, I told him to leave me alone, that his behaviour was upsetting me. He went into my brother's bedroom and showed my brothers pictures of naked women having sex and showing different pictures of both genders. It was horrible. I could hear my brothers laughing. He stood there with drink on him in their bedroom, telling them that he would show me the pictures as well. He came back into my bedroom talking, disturbing any possibility of having a peaceful nights sleep. He stood right in front of me and said "women have had to suffer putting up with men for centuries, not to mind childbearing. When they get married, they have to endure constant pain and misery."

Years Pass By

I wanted to see joy in my childhood days,
Much to accomplish,
I sought God's help
During difficulties
Days dragged like years
A prisoner in my own home
I wanted to see beauty and Joy
Smell the fresh air
Play in the garden
Like every child
Listen to voices, kids playing
Why couldn't I join?
Darkness falls, tried to enter Gods presence
I've used all the keys at the lock
Stared in the mirror with watery eyes
Asking, God why me?
Silence answered
My child you didn't knock

MY FATHER
WORKING AT HOME

As time passed, I felt my life was falling apart. I was approaching my 10th birthday and the sexual abuse was continuing. Living in a rural part of the Irish Gaeltacht in the West of Galway made it difficult for me to communicate with anybody regarding my father's behaviour. How would I explain it in Irish?

Some days, I walked home from school with my brothers. On other occasions, I walked with one of my friend's, Gemma, who was heading in the same direction. I used to walk up the laneway with my friend. Although I never discussed my father's behaviour with her, I found it therapeutic talking to her about life in general. She had a bubbly personality and was a year ahead of me in school. The journey was a little longer when I walked home from school with my pal, but the company was interesting. We generally parted at a fork in the road, Gemma taking the high road and Barbara taking the low road. I hated having to turn in the opposite direction to go home. As I continued walking, I spotted my house on the hill, overlooking a small lake.

As I entered my house, it felt cold. My father stepped out smiling and chatting away while making tea and slicing bread, asking me if my brothers were far behind me. I became aware that he was trying to find out how much time he would have with me on his own. I always replied that they were right behind me. If my father believed that they were not, he would generally try and touch me. My father's tirade began immediately. He started ranting, condemning men for their behaviour (I guess he forgot that he was one!) and how horrible they were. He complained that his own marriage was a curse and a horrible accident. I half-listened and thought to myself that the accident was him coming into this world.

BRIGHTER DAYS

Transparent thoughts
Fleeting in my mind
Leaves fall
My mind a blur
I'll get by
Longed for brighter days
Tears falling
I See the morning sun
I Hear the wind blowing
Life is challenging
I Count to ten,
Time passes, scars heal
I'll get by
Brighter days ahead.

I used to spend most afternoons at granny's, next door. I began to go to mass every Sunday, as my father never attended mass with us. My father used to stay home and peel the potatoes before we'd leave the house. He'd get the big pot prepared for stew. When we returned from mass, he would generally still be standing there peeling the potatoes. My mother asked him why it took him so long to peel a few potatoes. She told him that he was doing that job when she left the house. He replied that he had been doing other housework. "Do you not understand how tough this work is for a man being kept on his feet all the time?"

My father went out to the pub every weekend without fail. When my great granny passed on, my father refused to attend the funeral. My mother was obliged to attend the funeral on her own. She was very embarrassed because he wouldn't come along. She asked him what sort of excuse she could come up with to explain his absence as it was his relative and not hers' that had passed on. He shouted at her "Jesus Christ Almighty! Why are you making such of a big deal out of a funeral? She was old wasn't she. It was about time she passed away?"

He continued: "I won't go to the house. I will wait until the day they bury her. Tell them that I am sick. Why do you have to be honest with people?" He got dressed and went out to the pub as usual. The next morning, mam told him that people had been asking for him at the funeral mass and that it had looked strange to them that he had not attended the mass. My mother didn't like telling lies.

I began to lose interest in school. I could no longer hear the teacher talking because my mind wasn't allowing me to concentrate properly on what was going on. I also began to experience health difficulties. One Sunday morning, while attending Mass, I fainted. As I stood on the altar, I began to feel light headed. Suddenly my legs went from under me and my vision blurred. I awoke in a stranger's arms outside the church. I saw my mother standing in front of me with her hands on her face, wondering what had happened. Later that week, my parents drove me to our GP. I told the Doctor how I felt before I fainted. I was sent to him every week after that with the same symptoms. When our neighbours dropped in for a cuppa, they asked my parents if there had been any follow up done in relation to my fainting episodes. My parents told them that the Doctor had referred me to the local outpatient's clinic for further examinations.

One day, during a school Mass, I started to vomit. The head teacher stood up and rushed down to the back of the classroom to see what was wrong with me. I was embarrassed. All I could think of were the other schoolchildren and their parents watching me getting sick. I started crying. My uncle, who was standing beside me, told me not to worry and to stop crying. He reminded me that I didn't know I was going to get sick and that it had came on suddenly. For the next few days, I didn't attend school and was a frequent visitor to the Doctor's surgery.

Weeks later, I fainted again at Mass. I recall waking up in the arms of the same man from Camas who helped me the first time it happened. Mass was nearly over at this stage. My mother emerged from the church and ran over to where I was lying on the ground. The man who was holding me, looked up at my mother and asked who she was. My mother told him that she was my mother. He asked my mother if there was something wrong with me as this was not the first time this had happened. My mother told him that I was attending a Doctor with my condition. When we arrived home that afternoon, my father told mam that I should stay at home until my condition improved (he had his own reasons no doubt). My mother agreed. That was the end of me going to mass for a while. For the next few weeks, while my family attended Mass on Sunday mornings, my father entered my bedroom on several occasions. On the first occasion, he spoke to me about the night he had had in the pub the previous night. I was trying to keep myself covered with a blanket, so he couldn't come near me. It was no good – he would initiate a conversation and gradually ease his way onto the bed. Suddenly he told me to push up in the bed. He lay in beside me and forced himself on me. Again, I told him to stop. He wasn't interested in how I felt or the effect his behaviour was having on my health. He used my body against my will. I felt filthy afterwards and still didn't understand why my father was treating me in such a manner. After he finished, he resumed telling the same old stories, apologising and asking me questions like the last time - what effect was it having on me? - And blaming the drink, though he wasn't drunk at all. There was no alcohol in his system in the morning. I remember saying to him that it had nothing to do with alcohol, that he did this when he was sober. He told me that he was sorry and that he was going to stop. He then said, "I know this is why you get sick - it has a major effect on you. Would you be happy if I left you alone?"

He rambled on tirelessly, like a broken record, the same thing all the time. I was trembling at this stage, feeling sick and filthy. He began to talk about my mother's family. He was trying to get my mind off what he had done to me by bad mouthing my mother's family. At the time, my father threatened to drown me in the lake beside our house if I mentioned what he was doing to anybody. He pointed to the lake through the window. He also reminded me that my body would go down fast if he heard one word out of my mouth to anybody in the house or even granny's house next door. He mentioned that his family always reported everything back to him. He also told me that nobody would believe me. Suddenly, we heard the sound of our car driving up our lane towards our house. My mother and siblings were returning from Mass. My father ran out of the room quickly, saying as he went: "You know what I mean. Keep your mouth sealed and get that horrible sad face off and put on a bright face quickly for them. I'm warning you - don't give them anything to be suspicious of."

As soon as my mother and siblings entered the house, my father's demeanour changed immediately. He was very conversational asking who my mother had spotted at Mass. My mother's face brightened whenever my father behaved kindly towards her. My mother looked at my face and told my father that my complexion was quite pale. My father told her that I was fine. Mam commented that I was quiet. My father's demeanour gradually changed and he shouted "Jesus Christ, all mighty. What the fuck are you thinking, I didn't say a word to her". Later that evening, over dinner my father watched me picking at my food. Whenever I looked in his direction, I noticed a dirty look on his face. I began to daydream at the table. I noticed that the rest of my family were looking at me daydreaming.

The following day, I went in the car with my mother to visit her mother. My mother's mother was a hardworking lady and had a fondness for brewing poitin. She lived 9 miles from our house. I enjoyed listening to her interesting stories. She was a very interesting person and I seldom had a dull moment with her. Sadly, I didn't receive the opportunity to visit her as much as I would have liked. My father always ensured that I was kept at home to do whatever housework needed to be done.

Relations with my father's mother, who lived next door to us, were a little strained at the time. There were ongoing problems with my father's family at that time. My father's family were in the habit of constantly rowing with one another.

These rows could last for months, with members of my father's family not speaking to one another. Generally, the rows were quite childish. Sadly, when my father was rowing with one of his brothers or sisters, it impacted on the relationship I had with my relatives also. Due to the current row my father was having, I was unable to communicate with my aunt who I really liked. Although she was only 2 years older than me, we got on really well. However, at that particular time, my aunt would pass me in school silently. It was very sad when my father was on bad terms with his family that our entire family had to suffer because of his childish behaviour.

At the time I was having ongoing difficulties in school. Even though I had helpful friends in school, I was struggling to keep up with my studies. Much as I tried to keep joking away in my usual manner in front of my school friends, it became extremely difficult for me to continue with the pretence.

One day, one of my pals from school, who I walked home from school with, called to my front door. When she entered the house, my family, for no apparent reason, were awkward with her. While she was in the house, my siblings glanced in my direction, as if to say "why have you invited this person into our house." They didn't communicate with my friend and said very little until she left the house. She wasn't long gone when I overheard my father saying to my mother, "Where did she get the idea that she could bring her friends to the house?" My mother, easily intimidated by my father, merely looked at my father blankly. My father told me never to bring anyone to the house without his permission. I knew immediately that he would never give his permission for me to bring anybody to the house. My father suggested that my school friends might come to the house and steal things. At that stage, I didn't understand why my father didn't want any of my friends around our house. In his usual manner he said "If I didn't have any friends growing up as a child, why should you?" I looked at mam. It was unfair. She said "You must obey your father's rules". I couldn't answer back because I was afraid my father might hit me. That was the last time any of my friends came to the house.

CHRISTMAS

When Christmas arrived, my brother Niall and I decided to stay up and see if we could catch Santa delivering our presents. We sat quietly in our bedrooms for a couple of hours, but heard nothing. We became bored and decided to investigate as we had been told Santa could be very quiet when delivering presents. We jumped out of our beds and headed down the hall towards the sitting room to see if anything had been left under the tree. As we walked down the hall, we overheard our mother commenting to our father that we were awake and looking for our presents. We didn't care who knew we were out of bed. We were intent on discovering what Santa had left us. As we approached the sitting room, we could hear Tony calling us and asking if we had discovered any presents. We ignored his pleas and continued on our adventure. As I entered the sitting room, I spotted a doll in a pink walker. I became excited as I looked at the baby doll. I lifted her out of the walker and rushed around the sitting room kissing her. Niall had received the mountain bike that he had been longing for. We were the two happiest children in Connemara. When we had finished admiring our presents, we decided to tuck into the box of chocolates that had been left on the sitting room table. We stayed up all night playing with our toys. I was happy with my presents and the following morning at breakfast I asked mam what Santa had brought for my baby sister. Mam opened a towel and showed me a box of jelly sweets. She told me that Santa knew that little babies didn't have any teeth.

The day after Christmas, my father entered my bedroom and spotted me playing with the two dolls I had received from my godmother for Christmas. Without warning, my father grabbed my two dolls and told me that he was going to place the two dolls in the oven as they appeared to be shivering with the cold. I screamed at him to stop, but he ignored my screams and left my bedroom. I followed my father out of the room to the kitchen. He placed the two dolls on the tray my mother had used for our Christmas turkey and placed them into the oven. I screamed at him to stop, but he merely laughed. Moments later, he opened the oven and retrieved the melting dolls. They had been badly burnt. I tried to pull the tray away from him and rescue my dolls. Again, he laughed and showed the burned dolls to my brother. At this stage, I was crying. He then placed the tray on the kitchen table. When I tried to touch the dolls, my father started to laugh and said "You can't touch them now, you fool." Later that evening when my mother returned home, I told my mother what had happened. She told me that the dolls were destroyed and not to be whining.

I remember another Christmas we got up at 8am. My father shouted at us from his bedroom and told us to stop running around and turning everything upside down like robbers. We entered our parents bedroom and looked around to see if we could locate our toys. Our father's head emerged from under the blankets. He looked at Niall and said to him, "I know what Santa left for you. It's a bag of turf. I saw him early this morning." Niall became upset but continued his search. "If Santa did that, I will attack him when he puts his big fat legs down the chimney next year". Mam said "well I guess you all should go back to bed and not waste time looking for something that isn't there". My parents heard my brothers cursing, lifting the blankets, checking under every single bed in the house. Niall shouted 'wouldn't you think he would have put them in our bedroom instead of messing about, the same messing last year. It sickens me'.

Tony said "Niall did you hear the footsteps last night? I think I heard something." Niall replied "I don't know, but I noticed one thing the bloody bottle of coke that my mother left out of the fridge last night for him is empty on the table." 'No wonder he is so fat-- he left damn all for us. All he does is eat and drink. Niall replied. "Did you write a letter to him last night because I can't see that on the window sill". I told him if the letters were gone, that meant we got something. Tony was raging. He pulled the curtain and suddenly a big white bag fell out. He jumped with joy until he realised that it was Niall's name that was written on the bag. He said 'this means that my one isn't here as this was the last place to check. Frig that tinker,

Santa!' Niall didn't have time to listen to him because he was too busy playing with his toys. Tony jumped back up on his bunk bed, complaining, and found himself kicking a plastic bag under his feet under the blanket. He was annoyed and began shouting at Niall." I bet this is your bag of socks'. He asked Niall to remove them quickly. Tony pulled the blanket and noticed that it wasn't Niall's bag of socks at all, but his presents. He screamed with joy. We had a lovely dinner on Christmas day. My mother was a good cook. I found my own toys under a little mat outside my bedroom. They were well wrapped and as I pulled the wrapping apart, I spotted a green haired gollywog smiling at me. After I pulled the doll out of the bag, I spotted a colouring book and markers and a little blue dolphin that I could wind up. I was overjoyed with the presents. I told my mother that it was the same gollywog that the teacher had in a box at school and that the teacher allowed me to play with the Gollywog whenever I wanted to. I spent the rest of Christmas playing with my teddies and dolls.

After Christmas, I disliked taking down the decorations as I felt the Christmas warmth disappeared as the lights that used to shine from the Christmas tree vanished. I placed the little Angel back in the bag where mam told me to put all the decorations. I wanted her to leave them up. Granny came around to us that evening and told mam that she had made homemade butter for us. She was only around for a short time, but we received further visitors that day.

One night, a white shadow passed outside my bedroom door. I screamed loudly. I heard my brother Niall shouting from his bedroom. "Are you alright, Barbara." But, I guess he was too frightened himself to get out of bed. I didn't know what to say. I began to think that there was something wrong with my eyesight or that I was imagining things. With my plastic blue rosary beads in my hands, I started praying and crying and hoped that it would go away. I was afraid.

Later that night, I heard my father entering the house, having come from the pub, no doubt. I called on every saint not to let my father near my room. I was hoping that he wouldn't abuse me again. He walked into my bedroom and started shaking me, telling me to wake up. I pretended to be asleep. I could smell the alcohol off his breath. He said, "Now that you're going to Mass again in the morning, I don't get the chance to do anything. So get up." I was frightened. He realised that I was pretending to be asleep and pulled me by the legs out of the bed. He shook me to ensure that I was fully awake. He pulled up my night clothes and raped me on the bed. He told me to keep my mouth shut so that my mother couldn't hear anything that went on. I was helpless and didn't know how to endure the pain anymore. He was hurting me. I couldn't understand why my father was doing this to me again. I was in pain, tears flowing from my eyes, but he didn't stop. I tried to tell myself that it wasn't happening and that

I was only imagining that it was happening to me. I needed to escape. I was crying, the pain was excruciating. I was only ten years of age, thinking an animal wouldn't do this to its off spring. I begged him to stop. He continued and told me to be silent. This was the most horrible night of pain for me. When he was finished, he stood up, put his trousers on and rushed out of my bedroom. He was probably afraid that my brothers, who were sleeping in the room next to me, might have overheard him, as the walls in our house were quite thin. He left me there, crying. He then went out to the kitchen to cook something for himself.

Later that night, I went into the bathroom, locked the door behind me and washed myself. My father heard the water running in the bathroom for the shower. When I came out, he was standing outside the bathroom door. He asked me "Are you alright, Barbara?" pretending that nothing had happened earlier in the night. I somehow still felt dirty, even after having a cold shower. I was also shaking from the cold. I rushed down the hall to my bedroom. I didn't answer him. The following day in school was difficult for me. I was unable to stop thinking about my father's behaviour. I was also very tired, having been kept awake all night. How could I get rid of the feeling of emptiness inside me that was keeping me from having fun with the rest of my class mates, the way I used to in school. The following night, I told mam that I didn't want to sleep in that room on my own anymore. She replied "Don't tell me Barbara you're going to start on this again tonight." My mother finally relented and allowed me to sleep in the bed with her. I felt comfortable beside my mother and was able to sleep beside her. However, a couple of hours later, I heard a car coming up the driveway. I knew it was my father. I stared at the curtain and I could see the reflection of the car lights on the wall. But this time, because mam was there, I wasn't frightened. When my father entered the room, he asked why I wasn't in my own bed. Mam explained to him that I was upset and that I was seeing a shadow outside my room and that I couldn't sleep. He gave me a strange look. He got into bed, the other side of my mother. I felt safe.

The next morning, my father brought up the matter when the rest of my family were out of the house. He asked me about the shadow I had seen outside my bedroom. He appeared anxious. He told me not to be making up stories. I told him that I wasn't and that I had seen a shadow outside my bedroom. He told me that it must have been my imagination. I explained what I had actually seen. I told him that I used to see the shadow occasionally when I prayed. My father asked me to describe the shadow. I told him it was bright and appeared to be the shadow of a person. I told him that there was something on its head that I couldn't see properly. Then I screamed and it disappeared. I noticed it wouldn't come past the arch at the door. At that time, my father was constantly watching me. I felt suffocated.

Later that evening as my family watched television, my father called me back into his bedroom. As he pretended to sort the clothes in his wardrobe, he started giving out to me for no apparent reason. I asked him what I had done wrong. He told me to take that miserable looking face off while I was watching TV with my siblings. He told me that he would be watching me all the time (as if I didn't know). I wished at the time that he would get the hell out of the house and go abroad somewhere. I thought that when he had injured my mother in the past on two separate occasions that my mother was going to leave him. Sadly she lacked the courage. A social worker had visited my mother on one occasion and suggested that my mother might be better off if she were to leave her husband, my father. I had been excited at the prospect of putting as much space as I possibly could between my father and I. I encouraged my mother to leave my father, but didn't mention anything about the abuse to my mother at the time.

The following morning, I walked to school with my 2 brothers and my aunt Sally. She was 2 years older than me and I thought she was very intelligent. On our way to school, I mentioned to her that there was a possibility that we might be moving from the locality. She wasn't too happy. At that stage, I had little interest in how my aunt felt about the situation. I was happy to be moving away from my father. When I returned home from school that afternoon, my mother told me that she had ran away years ago to be safe from my father and that she had taken me and my two brothers with her to my Granny's house in Lettermore. I didn't know much about that time – I could hardly even remember what had happened as I was only a young child. My only memory was sitting on the floor with a bowl and spoon in my hand looking at granny's candle on the table with my brothers. For weeks, I honestly believed that my mother was going to take us away from my horrid father. Then one day, when I arrived home from school, my mother told us that we wouldn't be leaving after all. I was devastated. I couldn't believe it. I had been under the impression that I would have a happy normal life away from my father.

The weekend arrived. On Sunday afternoon, my mother and siblings were preparing for a day out. As I was the eldest girl, my mother asked me to remain at home and clean the house. She told me to clean the house, dress my two younger sisters, Grainne and Aoife, and keep an eye on the dinner that was cooking on the stove. She said she was heading out for a few hours and would return later that afternoon. I had no desire to be left on my own in the house with my father. I began to sweep immediately. I had the place spotless in less than 20 minutes. I put a red suit on my sister Grainne. I noticed that my mother was preparing to leave. All of a sudden my mother told me to mop the floor in case anybody should slip on a potato skin that had fallen on the floor. I mopped furiously. Finally, everything was in order. I said to my mother, "Mam, can I go with you now. I have everything cleaned." She told me that I had to stay at home and keep an eye on the dinner and take the clothes out of the washing machine and hang them on the line outside as soon as they were ready. I started to cry. My father gave me a peculiar look. My father then told my mother that he was going to go down the mountain for a walk and take a look at his cow. They left. I had to stay behind and wait. I stood at the window crying my eyes out. He watched them going out the gate in the car. "Jesus, Mary and Joseph, your crying there at the window, giving every signal that you don't want to be near me at home." I was too upset to speak. His voice got louder and I felt frightened by his big bully voice, knowing what was to come. He started telling me horrendous stories about what women had to put up with again. This time, my father's description became more detailed, focusing on the more violent and graphic aspects of marital relations. My father told me how men forced themselves on women and how this was an everyday occurrence. My father seemed to derive pleasure from relating these sordid events to me. I answered in an angry tone, "Why should women have to expect or accept this type of behaviour from men when they were married." He became angry when I answered him back. He was not used to that. His voice got louder by the minute, telling me that I was stupid and that I didn't understand. He shouted, "I suppose you think men and women get married for nothing............What do you think men do to women........ put them up on windowsills and look at them........Not at all you fucking lunatic." He worked himself into a state. I had become accustomed to this type of conversation by now. It wasn't right for me to be subjected to this. I wasn't able to deal with it. He called me into the bathroom. I will never, forget this horrible experience. He asked me to lean down on the bath. I refused and ran down towards the sitting room, crying. He screamed at the top of his voice and ordered me to come back. I was very frightened. He took the bathroom mats off the floor and placed it on the bath and told me to place my knees on it, that it wouldn't hurt my knees if I leaned on the mat. He made me lean on it and then he forced himself on me. This was a horrible experience. When he was finished he tried to talk to me and cheer me up. I can't seem to get this haunting image out of my mind. I was crying and he told me not to be like a child (but I was a child).

He sat in his room and called me in. By now, my face was red from crying. He had his green dressing gown on and was preparing to take a bath. He used to get ready early to go out on Sunday evening. I couldn't listen to him. I felt physically sick after what he had done to me. He started whistling, walking around the bedroom, becoming annoyed because he was tired of telling me to clear the miserable look off my face before my mother returned. He knew that she was due back. He began to give out about my mother's family. He was going on about how her family had kept him down soon after his marriage to my mother. He said that he used to go out with a suit and a tie on and they changed his life by telling him that he shouldn't wear good clothes. He rambled on tirelessly. He became angry when I didn't respond. I got the impression that he was trying to excuse his behaviour towards me by blaming my mother and her family. He continued saying that her family had destroyed his life. He also said that he had received no support from his own family. He blamed his "apparent" high blood pressure on his marriage to my mother and his continued bad relations with his own family. He claimed the Doctor had told him to take it easy with the stress and worry. The next minute, he raged about my mothers' grandmother who I loved. He said, "I would like to dig up her bones in the graveyard and smash her coffin. She was cruel to me, always telling me what to do". My recollections of this woman were totally at odds with my father's hateful comments. I felt my great granny was a kind, giving and considerate human being. Whenever I had the opportunity to visit her, God rest her soul, she was always kind and always waved to me when I was leaving. My father used horrible curses about her. Not alone that, he was looking towards the sky as he cursed. It was as if he believed somebody was going to answer him back. As he looked at the photograph of Jesus in the hallway, he cursed and asked that the sky would burst and harm those that he hated. I took a deep sigh and left the room. He called me back and warned me not to be mouthing to mam about what he had said to me.

Later that afternoon, my family returned. My father was in the bathroom getting ready to go the pub at 7pm. He generally went to the pub between 5.30 and 7.00pm, depending on which pub he was going to. I guess if there was money to be made on badmouthing and backstabbing, my father would have been a rich man. When my mother entered the house she commented that my face looked rather sad. She called my father and asked him if I was all right. My father rushed from the bathroom quickly and said, "What do you mean, sad face.....she's always like that." My mother said that I wasn't usually like that. He gave me a sign to cheer up when mam left the sitting room, to make tea. He told me to get that ugly face off and to smile in front of her. Thankfully he left after his tea.

A LETTER TO
ST MARTIN

My father came down to school the following day around lunchtime. He knew how upset I had been. As I played with my friends in the schoolyard, he called me over and said, "I've written a letter and put some money in it for Saint Martin. Here is the evidence. I wanted to show you before I posted it. I'm getting details and brochures about Saint Martin. I am showing this to you because it's proof that I want to stop doing this thing to you". I didn't believe him. He was trying to make me feel better again, trying to put a smile on my face. Too many times before I had heard this, that he would stop doing this, but somehow it always happened again. I wanted to believe him. I was only 10 years old. When he showed me proof of postage, I convinced myself that this was the end of it. Some of my friends were waiting for me at the gate to return. Several days later, I spotted the postman entering our garden. My mother who was in the kitchen also spotted him and walked out to greet him. I followed her out. The postman handed her several letters. When she opened one of the letters,

I noticed some religious brochures. I asked her if the holy brochures that had arrived were for her? She replied "No they are for your father. He ordered them from Dublin..... you know your father had a big operation on his scalp to try and make his hair grow back............he was hoping that if he said a few Novenas to St Martin that his hair would grow back." I realised immediately that my father had been lying. I felt upset and betrayed. Mam asked me. "What did you think it was for?" "Nothing." Liar, I thought. That's all I could ever expect to hear out of his mouth. Lies.

Drama And A New Teacher

A new teacher arrived in our school and took over 3rd, 4th, and 5th class in the middle room that we used to use for lunch. I thought the teacher was very kind and generous. She organised drama classes for us twice a week. At the time, I sadly didn't join in. There was too much sadness in me and I felt that I couldn't do anything entertaining with my class. My elder brother Tony took part in the drama group along with many of my classmates. In one play, Tony played the role of a priest and another local boy played the baddie. In one scene, the baddie goes to the priest and confesses murdering his granny. He told my brother (the priest) of all the evil sins that he had committed in his life. When I heard him saying the line "Father I have something serious to tell you, you won't like me for this, you won't believe me." Suddenly, I began to listen and concentrate on the play. I felt the character on stage was in some way showing me how to tell somebody about what was happening to me in my home. I felt the play momentarily removed me from the crisis I was in and from the negativity that had been strangling my life. The play was a success and went from our classroom to the Theatre in Galway City where they won first prize for acting in the National Schools category. I participated in dancing classes at school with my younger brother. We had classes in the headmaster's room on a couple of occasions. I thoroughly enjoyed dancing (and still do) and it was also great fun. We danced in groups as well as individually. My younger brother, I think, was the only boy who was learning how to dance. The girls occasionally made fun of him, but he didn't mind. He just kept on learning. Most of the time we used to have two ladies teaching us. It took a while on me to get the hang of it, though my neighbours, the three sisters, had no problem learning it. On our lunch break my friends used to give me dancing lessons in the shelter. Niall and I constantly practised. In the ensuing years, I won several trophies and medals as did many girls from my class.

At home, it was a constant struggle to try and attend dance classes on a Sunday. Fortunately, my aunt Sally, who lived next door was also attending classes which made it easier on us. On many occasions, I was in floods of tears, begging my mother to allow me to go to the dance classes. My father would complain about the cost of petrol (what was knew).

In the Summertime, my entire family worked on the bog turning turf. My mother turned turf with us, and my father told us to bring all the bags of turf down the hill to the main road. My mother walked in front of us carrying a heavy bag on her back. She stopped from time to time to rest. I hated working on the bog. My hands used to be filthy. After a while, my father bought a tractor. Whenever he worked on the bog, he used the tractor to carry the bags of turf. My father constantly complained about the amount of diesel the tractor used. I complained all the time about the weight I had to carry on my back and I used to be breathless by the time I reached the main road with the heavy bags on my back. I was too young to be carrying such heavy bags. I washed my hands in the small drain after working on the bog. On another occasion, my father told my mother that we needed to collect as many bags of turf as possible as the weather was going to deteriorate. I recall him saying to my mother in my presence "Let me know if they don't do much work, especially Niall. Don't give him a chance to sit around yapping. That's all he ever does". Our neighbours worked across the road from us on their own bog. I worked very hard on the bog and used to have backache afterwards. When I came home that night, my mother told my father that I did most of the work. I guess I was working very quickly with anger. I hated being there and just wanted to get the job done as quickly as possible. I couldn't face the place again. My father commented "I noticed that Barbara certainly works as hard as her Granny."

He shouted "How about Niall? Did he do much?" Mam told him that my younger brother Niall had worked hard on the bog as well. She knew my father would torment the heart and soul out of Niall if she had said anything different. My father treated Niall badly, and on occasion kicked him and told him on several occasions how useless he was. My father also told him that he was going to kick him out of the house by the time he reached his 16th Birthday. On another occasion, my father was working on a car. He was having difficulties fixing it and ultimately his frustration got the better of him. For no apparent reason, he punched Niall, who was helping him, in the face and in the ribs. This type of behaviour was not uncommon. On other occasions, my father threw heavy metal objects at Niall, such as monkey wrenches. On one occasion, he struck him on the head. Niall used to be too afraid to eat his dinner when my father was around. My father used to complain whatever my brother got for dinner. He claimed that it was too much for him to eat. He commented to my mother "How come Niall has so much on his plate?....I have nothing after a hard days work." Mam used to say "I didn't count the amount I put on anybody's plate. Why do you always pick on Niall and fight with him. What about the rest of them?" He used to say that Niall had a big mouth and that he would make him work in a factory near home at the age of 13 and that he would take all the money Niall earned. He went on about the food for a long time, saying that he was the only man that deserved a full meal and that Niall was getting the same amount on his plate as a hardworking man would get. My father said: "He should only be getting a little on the plate because the food will give him more power to be talking too much as usual?" Mam remained quiet whenever my father started complaining at the table.

I remember one night as I looked over the wall, I spotted my father and his brothers working on a car in their shed. They were drinking poitin. My father single-handedly lifted an engine from one car and placed it into another. My father and his brothers spent the entire night working in their shed. Although my father had talents, he refused to look for permanent employment and never seemed to use his talents in a productive manner. He misused his skills and seldom applied his abilities to anything productive. Whenever my mother suggested he travel to England for work, he said he never wanted to work as an employee and have someone else tell him what to do. On another occasion, my mother suggested to him that he should consider opening his own business. As usual, he agreed and did nothing about it.

One Sunday afternoon after dinner; my mother prepared to visit her family. My mother told me to get my two younger sisters, Aoifa and Grainne, dressed to go with her. I was anxious to get in the car to get out of my father's sight for the day. I tried to leave with them, but I overheard my father saying "No, no. She was bold during the week. Leave her behind. That should teach her a lesson. She was cheeky." My mother replied that she wasn't planning to bring me with her. I stood at the window crying until the car disappeared from view. Once it was gone, I ran around the house crying. I don't remember where my brothers were that day. My father began to curse at me. As I ironed my clothes, my father entered my bedroom and said "If I ever hear you telling anyone about what I have done to you, I will put a rope around your neck and throw you out the lake back the road…..Do you hear me?" This kind of talk frightened the living daylights out of me. I nodded. Although in the back of my mind, I knew that my father was trying to frighten me. I had been listening to these silly threats since I was 8 years of age. He was like a broken record. I hated the kind of language he used. While they were gone, my father abused me at home. It was in my own bedroom where I was raped. I stood near the window sill watching the sun go down, waiting for my mother to return. My father demanded that I put on a bright face. I felt trapped in his presence and locked inside. I felt so sick in the end, looking at the clock ticking, hoping the rest of my family would return home as soon as possible. I was obviously in a bad state because my father was a bundle of nerves, first screaming at me telling me to put on a bright face, then trying to console me telling me it would never happen again. I stood there looking very down, like a girl who hated the world. It was probably evident that something was very wrong with me or that something had been done to me. I felt that my life should end somehow. I said to myself, no not yet, the time is not right. Something was holding me back I was stunned, devastated, hateful, disgusted with myself again. I began to question myself inside and I developed anger within, wondering why this was happening to me. I felt ugly and unloved. When he had finished violating me, he spoke to me about his marriage with mam again. He said that it never worked out and that the reason he looked at me was because I was a pretty child. I turned around and asked "Does that give you a reason to do this thing to me." I thought he would fl are up on me but he didn't. He said "Your mother doesn't do anything for me anymore………I can't even make love to her, she puts me off ." I asked him why I had to put up with it. He replied "listen I'm never going to do this to you again, and if you fucking tell anybody do you see the lake that's back the road there. I will throw you out in it. Your body will never be found because I will put a block on your stomach and put a rope around your neck and I will make sure you will go down quicker." He warned me to keep my chin up when mam returned home and to have a bright face on when I would see my brothers and to be smiling and full of life around them.

The following morning, I had to face school again. It was very difficult. I couldn't understand anything anymore I felt my life was falling apart. I was scared and nervous. I came home that evening and my father started hitting Niall very hard in front of mam. My poor brother used to run around the house crying. One time, the school kids saw him. They saw my father chasing him around the fields with a Wellington boot. My brother was running around the field frightened. I thought the other kids would laugh at him, but they didn't. They felt sorry for him as they looked on in dismay, wondering what on earth was going on. On several occasions, my younger brother was badly beaten in front of mam. My mother, who was powerless when it came to my father's behaviour, sat there and looked while my father hit her son. She asked him politely on one occasion to stop, but he didn't. She couldn't do anything, only look across at my older brother Tony and I.

I remember one night when Niall got into bed. Mam, walked into his bedroom and noticed the purple bruises on his legs. She asked Niall who had put those marks on his legs? He was too frightened to say a word. I stood there listening at the door and I winked at Niall, trying to let him know that my father was listening at the door and not to say anymore because my father would belt him again. He said that he had fallen on the grounds outside. He looked scared and nervous when he saw my father behind her standing at the door. All of a sudden my father shouted, "What are yee all marching in his room for?" Mam said, "Well imagine if the GP saw those marks. What would he say?" My father said "There are only a few marks on him. That fella loves getting sympathy....he probably got those cuts on his legs because of his mouth." He gave my brother a dirty look and walked out of the bedroom.

Mam discussed it with my elder brother and I in the kitchen. I told her "Do you remember Niall said that he fell on the ground? He didn't! My father did all this." I noticed whenever he used to hit my younger brother that he used to give me dirty looks as if to say "I can do the same to you girl".

I remember he hit me on a few occasions, but it wasn't that bad. He was doing worse things to me. What could be worse than rape? I'd much rather he beat me than rape me. It would be easier to tell, it would save a lot of embarrassment.

In the month of September, my father told me that he was going fishing on the lake. What a place to go fishing, I thought. "I wonder how deep the water is? They say when you see flowers or leaves on top of the water it means that it's very deep." he said. In the end, my two brothers and I had to accompany him. When we reached the lake, Niall, Tony and I sat beside our father as he fished in the lake.

Moments later, my father called us over. He had a rope in his hand. He then put the rope around Niall's waist and told Niall to jump into the water. Niall looked at him in disbelief but was too afraid to do anything other than comply with my fathers orders. "I will put you under the water for a few seconds to see what it feels like." He said. Niall then jumped into the water. After a couple of minutes, my father told Niall that he could get out of the water. Niall was shivering at this stage. My father then looked at me, placed the rope around my waist and told me to jump into the water. It felt strange. As my head went under the water, I began to cough as the cold water entered my mouth. I then felt the wet rope tightening around my waist. It felt very uncomfortable. When my head finally re-emerged above the water, I could see my father laughing. It was an eerie sight. He then pushed me down into the water for a second time. Again, the cold water rushed into my mouth. This time, I swallowed the water and began to cough. I was very frightened. When I returned to the surface, I was coughing water out from my lungs. My eyes were also sore and I was quite cold. I looked pleadingly at my father who merely laughed. He then lowered me into the water for a third time. This time I began to cry and was terrified as I couldn't swim. When he finally lifted me back into the boat, tears were streaming down my cheeks. My father made some sarcastic remark to my brothers as I stood there shaking. When I returned home later that evening I told my mother what had happened.

My father also had the habit of cutting my hair very short, like a boy's, which I greatly disliked. He also cut my two sisters hair very short as well. I remember returning to school after the weekend after having my hair cut. The other children in the class laughed at my hair. One girl from the neighbourhood stood up realising how badly I was affected by these remarks. She told me to ignore nasty comments from other people and that they were jealous. Some people asked who had cut my hair. I told them all that my father had cut my hair. Once a boy, outside the school at lunch, laughed at my hair. I ran into the toilet crying. I didn't come out for twenty minutes. That week, our priest read Mass in our classroom. I will never forget the words he said: "It doesn't mean if a person's hair is short that they look different from anybody else and it doesn't mean that a person is ugly". He probably noticed that I was very shy and uncomfortable about my hair. There was a big crowd there from the other two classrooms.

My life began to change at school. I started fighting with some of the girls. Maybe I was being bullied because I was so vulnerable over what was happening to me behind closed doors. We used to fight over silly things, but I guess that was part of growing up. Those days, I used to listen to some of my friends from my class saying that they were on holidays with their parents and doing everything during the summer. I had little in common with them. They told me about the lovely gifts their parents used to buy for them, such as colouring pencils and bits and pieces for school. I used to sit there and look at them and think that they were so lucky having wonderful parents.

I began to spend a lot of time on my own, sitting on the stairway, removed from my fellow classmates. I kind of liked that in a way, as I could spend time thinking. One afternoon, one of the girl's parents who came to our school walked over to me and asked me to join the other girls in the yard. I remember she was trying to cheer me up because she had noticed that I had been sitting staring into space, not knowing whether I was coming or going. I told her that some of the boys were laughing at me and telling me that my hair looked ugly like a boy. She told me not to listen to them. When I returned home in the afternoon, I complained to mam about my hair. I told her that it was too short and that people in school were laughing at me. My mother offered little support. She merely complained to my father of having to listen to me complaining about my hair. My father then told me not to be mentioning my hair to my mother as my constant whinging was driving her mad. My father told me to stop worrying about my hair and that my hair had to be cut. Another time, when my hair began to grow a little, he got a chair and told me to sit on it, outside the shed in our back garden. He began to cut my hair very short. Tony, came around and pleaded with my father to leave my hair and not to cut it. Tony said my hair looked nice and that it didn't need a haircut. As usual, my father ignored his comments and continued with the scissors. My lovely curls dropped to the ground. Tony still pleaded, but to no avail. It didn't matter to my father how it looked .There was nobody going to put ideas in his head. He just wanted me to look ugly in school. He began to do the same job to my sister's hair. As soon as their hair passed their shoulders, out came the scissors. They weren't happy about it either. I could see they were upset. But what could we do?

One afternoon, my godfather, who lived next door to us, dropped in for a chat. He spotted me at the back of the hall standing on the mop bucket. He started laughing and asked my mother how I managed to keep balance on both sides of the bucket. My mother told him that I got up to every sort of devilment.

On another afternoon, as my siblings and I watched TV, my father who had been sleeping on the settee woke up and screamed at us to lower the volume. He told Niall to go and find a pen. As we sat in the sitting room waiting for Niall to return, our father became more impatient. After several minutes, Niall finally returned with a tiny pencil. My father began to complain almost immediately. "Jesus, Mary and St Joseph, look at the size of the bloody pencil he gets me. What do you have in your satchels? Apples instead of school books and pens". My father stood up and walked over to the TV and drew a little line beside the volume button. He turned to us and said, "While ye are all sitting there, I might as well give you a warning in case there is any misunderstanding. If the volume goes above the mark I have just drawn on the TV, I will blow the television up in the field with the rest of the trash. We never had televisions when I was young. We had to do without it, so why do you lot need it?" After that it became impossible to enjoy the TV as we could barely hear the person on the TV speaking, the volume was so low. It was like watching news for the deaf. It was the same with the radio. Whenever I got the chance I had the radio blaring.

As young children, my brothers and I had watched our granny and our mother making jam. During the Summer, my brothers and I quite often went out and picked blackberries when the weather permitted. My mother knew that all of us had sweet teeth. When we returned to the house with the blackberries that we had picked, we immediately began to make jam with them. We always added more sugar than we should have. Our mother generally watched us, but said nothing. We thoroughly enjoyed the experience and gradually became experts in the field of making jam.

One day, when I returned home from blackberry picking with my brothers, I joined my younger sister in the back garden where we usually played in the sand. My younger sister Grainne had a very pretty doll that we played with. We used to put water in the doll's mouth and feed her. I used to tell my sister 'the doll had eaten the sand'. Grainne was about six years of age at the time, I told her that the doll needed a lot of water because of the hot weather. I thoroughly enjoyed sitting out in the sun, and playing with my sister. Suddenly my sister and I spotted a plane in the sky. It seemed that it was coming in our direction. We both waved our hands in the air. In a matter of time the plane had approached us. Mam opened the window and told us "the plane will come closer if you keep jumping up and down. They will think that you need to be rescued." It was wonderful. The plane flew right over us. My sister then went in the house to get more water for the doll. While my sister was getting more water in the house for the doll, I found a broken bottle in the sand. I broke it into pieces and scattered the broken pieces all over the sand. My sister returned and walked right on the sand with her bare feet. Immediately she began to cry. I spotted blood on her feet. I felt terrible. My Grandmother appeared almost immediately and lifted my younger sister up in her arms and carried her into her house. Inside, my granny gave my sister an orange as she put a bandage on my sister's foot. My sister stopped crying almost immediately. Granny was very good when it came to things like that. She genuinely cared for us!

At this time, one of my father's old school friends returned home from England to live in our neighbourhood with his wife and children. His children began to walk to school with my siblings and I. They were excellent company on our journey to school. Sadly, at the time, I wasn't in the mood to play with any of them. They made every effort to include me in whatever game they played. However, I generally refused as other thoughts preoccupied my mind. One morning, as I sat on the school wall with my brothers and Jack, the English boy, my eldest brother asked us all if we would like to play a game. Tony suggested that I could watch as I wasn't too well at the time. Jack, asked me what was wrong with me. As he spoke to me, I began to cry. He looked very upset. I realised he was only trying to be friendly. Tony, walked over and told him that I had problems with my health.

One day, while sitting in our kitchen, I questioned my mother as all kids do. My mother became angry and accidentally prodded me with a kitchen knife that she was using to cut the meat. I began to scream out loud. "Look I'm bleeding." 'Shhhh!' she said. "Put a bandage on it quickly so the rest won't come in and see it'. She opened the first-aid box and pulled out a bandage and scissors along with some white tape. "I didn't know that the bread knife could cut like that" She said. That evening, I felt a painful sensation in my arm.

The following day, my complexion was very pale in school. Some of my classmates asked me what was wrong with me and why I looked so pale?' I told them that I was feeling unwell. On our way home from school that afternoon, my brothers and I met our mother who asked us if we would like to go to the Circus in Carraroe. We jumped in the car. None of us had ever been to a circus before. As soon as we arrived at the circus, I spotted a few kids from my school there already. When I looked at the stage, I could see a multitude of colours. It was like multi-faceted crystals in a sun-lit window. I could see its light-splitting prisms making beautiful rainbow patterns. Some of the clowns were wonderful performers. I could hear some of the people laughing but I found it difficult to laugh. All of a sudden, I spotted a white bandage on the clown's arm while he was dancing around the ring. I remembered that was the same colour bandage that I was wearing on my right arm. I was very sad sitting there in deep thought. I only reacted to some of the more humorous things they were doing. The clown drove an old bonnetless car into the ring. I remembered that my father had a car before without a bonnet. The show went on for two hours and was thoroughly enjoyable.

During the winter when the weather was bad, our parents let us stay home from school. My siblings and I watched cartoons like "Tom & Jerry". My father used to say "I don't want to waste bloody petrol bringing them down the road to school. It's not on". The school was only a few hundred yards down the road from our house. It wasn't long before our headmaster realised why we weren't attending school. He turned around and said to the class "I notice the Naughton's only attend school when the weather is fine". The headmaster contacted our parents and insisted that we attend school. He said that we should be driven to school, whatever the prevailing weather condition.

An old man used to come to our house at the same time with a black plastic bag on his back. He was a homeless man and not known to anyone living in that area. In the beginning, I used to get really frightened when I saw him approaching our gate, dishevelled, unshaven and hungry, his hair all over the place. I found it scary looking at the holes in his shoes and his open shoelaces. I used to hide behind the door. As soon as the old man approached our house, my mother told me to open the door for him. At the time, there was coloured glass in our front door. When I opened the door, I stood right behind it so I wouldn't have to look directly at his face. He saw my shadow behind the door and stood there wondering if he should come in as it appeared that there was no one there to greet him. My mother then called from the kitchen and asked me if I had opened the door. However, I was afraid to speak in case the old man heard me. He called out to my mother who came out to the front door to greet him. As I looked up at my mother, she returned my look with anger all over her face. After a while, I became used to the routine. I noticed my mother used to boil an egg and cut slices of bread for him. When I spotted him approaching our front door, I ran out to the back garden and remained there until I heard the front door opening again and knew that he was leaving. When he left, I returned back into the house. My aunt next door was as frightened as I was. Whenever she saw him approaching the gateway, she screamed and hid behind the wall. She exclaimed oh Jesus, there is the gollywog. One day, as I returned home from school, I discovered the old man sitting on our couch with my two brothers. He was reciting poetry. I felt relaxed and listened to a poem he recited about a dog. After a while he stopped coming to our house. I missed the excitement we had hiding on him. My mother told us that she heard on the radio that a car had hit him. We were sad on hearing this news.

One morning, as I walked down the hill on my way to school with my brothers, my younger brother Niall and I were nattering on about money. Tony, looked at us lost in thought, wondering what we were discussing. Suddenly, we spotted a plastic bag in a hedge at the side of the road. Niall opened it and exclaimed "Jesus it's amazing what you can find at the side of the road". Niall opened the bag and several coins spilled out. We picked up the coins and began counting. Tony looked at us in shock and asked us how we knew that there was money in the bag and why we had been discussing money that morning. We looked at each other and wondered. Tony said 'Isn't that very strange. It must be a miracle or did Niall have a magic wand. There are so many kids walking up and down this street everyday and none of them ever mentioned finding money at the side of the road'. We told him that we did not steal it and that we had no idea how it came to be there. Tony looked at us, laughed and told us that we should leave the money there and retrieve it on our way home from school that afternoon. Tony said: "If you said that you didn't know where it came from, father would kick you".

That afternoon, on our way home from school, we retrieved the money from the hedge. As soon as we reached home, Tony told my mother and father about our good fortune. He explained how Niall and I had discovered the money. Mam said "Well the lord save us. I noticed there was money missing from the wardrobe the other day". Tony and I became confused and wondered what was happening. We had no idea who was the actual owner of the money. My parents took the bag of coins and told us to forget about the incident. I instinctively knew that neither my father, or mother were the actual owners of this money. My father concocted a story about losing money from his wardrobe. My mother concocted a story about having won the money at bingo. My brother and I knew that both my parents were lying. My mother took the bag of coins and began counting. As soon as my mother began counting the coins, my father, changed the subject immediately. "Well I hope it's all there. I'm sure that I had some money in my wallet. I'm certain that I had a jar of coins under my bed." he continued.

"Barbara Naughton, aged 7, in National School"

The Naughton's Family Home, Camus, Co. Galway

Barbara and One Of Her Teddy's

MONEY MISSING
FROM THE JAR

One night, our next door neighbour visited us. My mother sent us to bed early so that we would be up for school the following morning. We lay in bed listening to see if the lady from next door was still around. At the time, our parents seldom bought sweets for us. My mother told me that they would damage our teeth. That night, we opened mam's wardrobe and spotted a jar full of coins that she had won at the bingo. I looked at Niall. We both laughed with happiness. Our dream had been answered. "I bet you she doesn't know how much is in the jar. It's full of coins and she wouldn't have the time to count all that,' Niall said. He opened the lid and saw lots of 2p and some silver coins. We burst out laughing as soon as the lid popped open. Mam shouted from the sitting room and told us to go to sleep. But we were going on an adventure. We opened the window in my parent's bedroom and managed to sneak out the window. Niall and I were nervous in case my mother opened the sitting room door and caught us going out. It was late at night. We both walked down the hill encouraging each other. We imagined that the shop would be open late. However, when we reached the shop at the bottom of the hill, it was closed. The two of us stood there banging at the door. My brother told me to keep knocking as the people inside were generally slow coming as they were quite old. We kept on knocking, but no one replied. As we were coming out the gate, we ran into our aunt coming from her neighbour's house. We got the shock of our lives and so did she. Her eyes widened when she saw us. She asked, "Where the hell are you going?" We were speechless. Eventually, we told her that we had dropped down to the shop. She laughed and told us that the shop was closed. She kept looking back at us as we ascended the hill towards our house. 'Wait till I see your mother tomorrow'. The two of us had been hoping that she wouldn't tell on us. We managed to get back in the window without any difficulties. All that night my brother and I were worried about what our aunt was going to say to our parents. My brother said "we can tell mam that our aunt imagined that she spotted us. Who is going to believe that kids our age go out at that time of the night. Mam will tell her that she put us to bed and that our aunt was imaging it all".

The following morning, as Niall and I sat on the sitting room couch the sun shone through the window. I heard my mother going out to water the flowers. "Oh the lord save us. Please ensure that she doesn't go near the geraniums near the wall or she will be facing granny's house. Our aunt might come out and tell her about last night" my younger brother Niall said. I rushed out, but before I got the opportunity to stop my mother, my aunt had called her over. As usual, my aunt spoke at the top of her voice. My aunt was one of those people who enjoyed other peoples' misery and inflicting misery on others. I heard her relating the events of the previous night to my mother. I ran into the house and told my brother what had happened. As we sat there, we wondered if it would be easier to stay indoors or go out to our mother and face the music.

My mother rushed back into the house and asked us what we had been doing outside of the house at that hour of night. We told her that we didn't go out at all. She grabbed the little brush and hit us with it on the legs. I saw my aunt standing at the wall roaring laughing, tears streaming from her eyes. My brother put many curses on our aunt that day.

Meaning Of The Church

The following day, my father sat on his double bed, sewing his pants. Tony, my little sister and I were in the bedroom, sitting on the bed. All of a sudden, we heard a stream of bad language from my father's mouth, cursing about the needle sticking in his hand. We heard him saying "Fuck the lot of you up there in heaven. I know you're doing this to a man deliberately. I'd love to put a bomb up there and kill all the fakers in heaven. There is nobody up there." My sister Grainne burst out laughing. My brother looked at her and told her to remain silent as he wanted to listen to my father. As we sat in the bedroom, my father's tirade continued. He said "one of these days I will send that holy picture flying off the wall that's constantly staring at me. It seems to be causing too many problems. It's cursed". He shouted 'I hope that an awful thunder storm will come and make pieces of the planet'. I looked at my sister who was holding a pillow on her mouth, tears cascading from her eyes with laughter. He started shouting and making noises like he was throwing things around the bedroom. I got an awful shock listening to him praying for badness. I hoped that the saints would burn him in hell. What shocked me was to hear him speak ill of the saints after ordering brochures from Saint Martin De Porres office in Dublin hoping and praying for his hair to grow back. He had also received scapula and medals. He had attached the gold medals around a chain on his neck.

Later that afternoon at dinner a row erupted between my mother and father about the church. My mother asked my father to stop criticising the church in front of the children. My father replied that the church and all those who worked in it were all crazy people, especially the priests. He told my mother that the church was a money racket and that the priests didn't seem to work but still lived in nice houses. He asked my mother where the church got its money. My mother merely ignored him and left the kitchen. The following morning as we were heading out to Mass, my father asked my mother why she was wasting petrol going to Mass. My mother told my father not to put us against religion because he had no belief in anything. As we followed my mother out the door, my father said "There is a war going on in this house. Rushing to mass because of the priest.............. he is not forcing anybody to hurry there". My mother replied "Jesus, Mary and Joseph, what kind of belief is that? Keep your voice down and don't have them listening to that kind of talk". He shouted at my mother as we made our way out to the car "if the church is so good to you, why do you have so many problems". As I sat in the car, I was glad that I didn't have to remain in the house with my father that morning. Mass was the only place that I could go where he couldn't touch me.

A few weeks after that, I woke up one morning with severe abdominal pains. I called my mother into my bedroom and told her about my stomach pains. My mother told me that she would call the doctor immediately. My father merely walked around the place with a guilty look on his face. My mother then searched for the Doctor's number in the phonebook.

While my mother was searching for the phonebook, my father pulled up my top and said, "Look, she has no breasts. She is so flatchested." My mother turned on him and asked "what are you doing, acting like a maniac, pulling Barbara's top." When she found the doctor's number, my mother told me that she would head across the road to one of our neighbours who had a telephone and ring the Doctor. As she headed out the door, my father told my mother not to tell the lady across the road what the calls was about. When the doctor arrived he gave me some tablets.

A few days later, I was home alone with my father. He called me into his bedroom and asked me to lie down beside him. I felt the shivers running through me with disgust. The thought of stabbing him kept running through my mind. All I could think about was the knife. Suddenly, I heard a knock on the front door. I answered the door. It was an elderly man from the neighbourhood who had dropped in for a social visit. My father pretended not to be home. At the same time, he began to make silly whistling sounds. He called me and told me to get rid of the visitor as quickly as possible and not to offer him any tea. His whistles and voice could be heard at the front door. The old man knew there was somebody else in the house. He could hear my father calling me. I was embarrassed. The man had asked "Is any of your family around?" I replied 'no' even though I knew very well that the elderly man had heard everything my father had said. He was cruel. Eventually, the elderly man said that he had to leave as he had a few things to do. I hated when he left as I knew my father would try and abuse me again. My father called me into his room. I told him that I didn't want to go into his bedroom. He kept insisting. He shouted "I'm dumb and deaf and I can't hear what you're saying. You're mumbling out there in the hall at the heater. Nobody can hear you with your big ugly mouth." I didn't really want to take on board what he had said, but it was disturbing me. He called me again and kept insulting me, saying 'you're ugly, disgusting looking, that's why I was abusing you all along. It's good enough for you…' I felt angry when he said that. I grounded my teeth with anger. I made fists as he made those hurtful remarks. But it felt like being raped again. The words he used against me were sufficient to scar me. I thought that was the reason he had been hurting me. Suddenly my brothers arrived home. He told Niall to hit me. His idea of sport was to ask Niall to start a fight with me. He used to get my brother worked up so that he would slap me. It pleased him to poison us all and to turn us against one another.

One day, as Niall and I skipped outside our home, Tony, my eldest brother drew white boxes on the ground. He put the numbers one to nine in different boxes and told us to jump in the boxes that he chalked. The game was called hopscotch.

I tried to work hard at it, attempting to avoid certain boxes whilst trying to keep my balance as I jumped from box to box. We learned that game in National school. We used to watch the older kids playing it all the time. Whenever we were bored at home, we played that game or skipped to pass the time. We had a great time playing that game. It kept my mind off other matters. Niall and I went in the house after a while and climbed onto the sink to look in the cupboard to see if there was anything nice in it. We spotted a sweet cake. We asked my mother if we could have a piece. I told her that the cake was in little crusts and that I'd love to eat it. 'Go ahead the two of you. You can finish it outside. Its a gorgeous day", she said. We were so happy to have the cake. We were only allowed to eat sweet things at the weekend. Niall and I sat in the field enjoying the cake. The birds kept flying around us for food. We were so happy that my father wasn't around to shout at us. We felt at ease while we were eating the sweet cake.

Another day, I remember I wanted to get some biscuits but we weren't allowed because they were specially kept for visitors. My brother and I stole them and ate them in the field.

I made little crusts and gave the birds some of the crumbs. Mam called us in and said "Jesus, Mary and Joseph I was so embarrassed. When I made Tea for the lady next door, the Digestive biscuits were missing". We blushed and looked at each other. She knew immediately what had happened. She warned us not to do it again.

BLACKIE

We had a lovely black and white dog called Blackie and I enjoyed feeding him. He would wag his tail whenever I fed him. My father hated the dog. My mother had been the one who had encouraged him to get the dog. We never had any pets before. Blackie was our first dog. Mam made a little shed for the dog beside our home. I used to go out everyday after dinner and give him the potato skins. As far as I can remember my father never bought dog food. My father never had any interest in animals. The only way my mother convinced him to have a dog was to say that it would keep the cows out of our garden. A dog would be ideal to keep them away. My parents also got some hens from friends. Niall and I enjoyed feeding them crushed bread.

One day, as I walked around the house to feed the hens, I spotted my father in the garden with his brother. My father held one of the hens and cut his little head off with a pocket knife. I ran into the house crying to my mother and told her to go out and to stop my father from hurting the hens. She told me 'that's what people do all the time for food'. I told her that I loved animals and didn't want the lovely hens to be hurt. My mother walked out and stood at the side of the house and watched him. She told him that I was upset over it. A wicked smile crossed my father's face as he chopped their heads off . I remember my father wanted to get rid of Blackie. My father claimed that poor Blackie had been useless around the house. But my uncle said that granny would miss him. However, my Father's mind was made up. He tied the dog to the back of the car and drove towards the cave. The dog tried to free himself, but to no avail. I was extremely upset. I stood at the side of our house looking at the dog being dragged along, struggling to stay on his feet with a rope tied around his neck. I wanted to believe that he would change his mind, but he didn't. Later that evening, he did the same thing to my granny's dog next door. He stopped the car in the middle of the road and pulled out fast. As I stood at the back of the house I noticed my father looking in the side door mirror on the passenger seat. The car window was down, and laughter could be heard coming from within the car. No doubt, my father was finding the whole experience very amusing. He laughed loudly as the dog tried to free the rope from his neck. I stood at the side of the house and watched him making fun of the poor animal. My mother told him that I had gone out to see him going back with the dog. 'The girl couldn't believe you were going to do that on her,' she said. All he said was "that's Blackie now for you. He is dead now. He didn't float on top of the water for long, he went down quickly".

My young sister cried when she heard this and banged her bedroom door. My father felt a little guilty and promised to buy her sweets, but none for the rest of us. When my father returned, he gave my younger sister a large bag of sweets. He told her that he had to get rid of the dog as the dog's hair was aggravating her asthma. My sister Grainne was not convinced, but tucked into the sweets and chewed away to her heart's content.

An old fellow came around from the neighbourhood who always smoked a pipe. He was such of a lovely person and wonderful company. He visited us on occasion. He was one of the few people that my father didn't talk about. When the elderly man visited he enjoyed listening to my brothers and I talking about school life and our friends. He asked if we received potatoes in school, 'as he used to get when he went to the same school as a boy". My brothers talked to him about boxing and told him that they would like to take up boxing as a hobby.

Most of the boys from their class and other boys from the local area joined them in the local youth club. They used to have lots of activities going on in the local hall, including indoor soccer and basket ball. They also held discos there.

In general, I had to complain endlessly to my parents before I was permitted to go there. My father tried at all times to keep me home. My elder brother was learning how to play the accordion at school. He played tunes he learnt from the elderly man who used to visit us. My father had a habit of spending days on the toilet seat playing the accordion. Sometimes he sat on his bed playing it for a couple of hours in the afternoon. He never really played much in public. Tony used to come home with a notebook to help him learn more tunes. My father told him that he was unable to read notes and that he preferred to play by ear. Tony noticed that my father was able to play the two rows on the polo soprano accordion that he had. He seldom explored his talent. His mind was too focused on badness.

One evening, when I arrived home from school, the old man who smoked the pipe was sitting in our house chatting to my mother. I was always happy to see him. I said hello to the old man, threw my bag on the couch and ran out into the garden. While I was playing in the garden, I bumped my forehead off a big rock. When I put my hand to my forehead, I noticed there was blood on my hand. I screamed with fright and ran into my mother who was in the sitting room. She looked at my forehead and immediately stood up and brought me into the kitchen where she dabbed my forehead with a damp sponge. She then dried my forehead with a towel. The old man came into the kitchen, a look of concern on his face, and told me not to be afraid. Moments later, I returned to the garden and kicked the nasty rock for hurting me.

Later that week, my father went to his mother's house next door. There were three men already there from the neighbourhood. My father called them over to a shed across from Granny's house. He told them that he was going to set a trap for the birds. They were confused, not understanding what he intended. He placed a piece of cheese in the trap and left it on top of the shed. As the four men stood there, they gradually became bored waiting for the birds to come down and grab the cheese. My father decided to replace the piece of cheese with a piece of bread. This time a bird approached the snare. As the bird tried to pull the piece of bread out of the trap it got his legs caught in the trap. My father started roaring laughing and he took the trap down. He continued laughing as the poor creature struggled to walk. I was standing outside my home watching this carry on. I felt sorry for the poor bird. My father stood over the poor creature as it tried to fly in vain. When my father released the bird from the trap, it ran around trying to lift its wings and fly. It became apparent that the bird had damaged its wing. The more the poor bird struggled, the more laughter I heard from my father.

Inspector Of Taxes

On another occasion, my father asked his friends to give him some medication so that he could give it to his father's donkey. He gave the poor donkey half a bottle of antidepressants tablets. After a few minutes, the donkey fell on the ground. The following morning, when his father came out, he discovered the donkey lying on the ground motionless. He stood there surprised, wondering what had happened to his donkey? My father stood at the wall and laughed. Granddad asked 'Jesus do you know what happened to the donkey? That's very unusual for that to happen I wonder how did it happen?' He kicked the donkey and tried to wake him up. But the poor animal was long past caring.

Another day, when my mother had gone to Galway for the day, my father sat on his bed writing letters. I knew that there was little chance that my father was sitting down doing something productive. I asked him what he was doing. He replied "Well I was going to call you and show you the technique for handling people that you hate and how to take revenge and bring them down to their knees where they belong."

He said "There is this lady across the road who makes me sick. She is always in here blabbing away about things and never has a good word to say about me to your mother. She has lodgers in her other house that's in her son's name. I will stop that happening very quickly. I know she is also on the dole. However, the pen is mightier than the sword". I asked him what he was going to do. He replied "I'm writing a letter to the Inspector of Taxes. This is his address in case you need to contact him in Galway. Do you see now what I mean?" I told him that the inspector might have more important matters to deal with. He shouted "He will listen. He has a boss over him. I will go to the highest mark to nail him if he fails to do his duty". He told me that the woman had to be straightened out and this was the man who would straighten her. I couldn't believe what I was hearing. I was standing there trying to make sense of it all. I wondered why my father spoke nicely to the woman whenever she came to visit us and did all this behind her back. He used to be nice to her husband too. I asked him what was the purpose of doing all this. He got very annoyed with me and replied "are you stupid or something. A person is not allowed to be signing on the dole and working, especially that lunatic who lets one of her houses and gets the dole. That's illegal". As he walked around the house whistling, his face was red with rage and he shouted that it wasn't fair for the innocent people out there to be suffering.

He then wrote a letter to the inspector about a man who lived in another neighbourhood who happened to be an apparent friend of his. He said that man had an awful cheek coming over to Kinnvarra cutting seaweed in our patch and that the man needed to be taught a lesson. He told me that he wanted to keep all the seaweed in the vicinity to himself. He disliked when others used to cut seaweed from "his" patch. He said "there is plenty of seaweed near his own place, but he is so greedy going back the road to our cave. I know how to deal with people like him. This is the man you write to whenever you have a stone in your sleeve for somebody." I thought to myself that he should have been a Private Investigator as he had such a methodical approach to his work. If he made an error while writing, he would rip up the page and start again.

At least he would be getting paid for reporting people as it seemed to be his ongoing profession. He told me he would post the letter later that day. He said that the Inspector should receive it the next morning. He shouted "Don't you realise I'm doing the Inspector a favour. As a matter of fact, I'm doing his job for him. He should be doing this himself." He was elated and excited when he finished the letters.

I remember another occasion when my mother's sister dropped over to visit us. My mother was trying on clothes for a wedding that she had been invited to the following day and her younger sister was helping her. As they discussed the wedding, I decided to make myself a cup of tea. As I walked towards the kitchen, I noticed that our bathroom door was open. An uncomfortable thought entered my mind, a conviction that either something had happened or was going to happen. It was like a vibration in the chest area, it was a horrible sensation. As I approached the bathroom, I heard my father's voice. I returned to the sitting room and told my mother that my father had returned home. My mother told me to tell my father that the wedding was starting at 12 o'clock the following day. I returned to the bathroom. As I entered the bathroom, I spotted my father placing a plastic bag on the windowsill in the toilet. He then pulled a bundle of paper money from the plastic bag and began counting it. When he spotted me, he asked me. "What the hell are you doing standing there sneaky looking?" I didn't know what to say. I told him that my mother had sent me in to tell him what time the wedding was starting the following day. I knew without being told that he had robbed this money. My father told me to keep my mouth shut and that if I opened my mouth to anybody that I would suffer. He told me that I was the only person who knew about the money.

On another occasion, my father's sister came to baby-sitter. My father's brother arrived at the house and began to fight with his sister in the hall. The next thing I heard her screaming. I ran out with my brothers and saw blood flowing from her nose. I was disgusted with her brother for hitting her. I thought to myself what a family. I always felt there was something dysfunctional about my father's family. When I told my mother about the incident the following morning, she explained to me that she always had difficulty getting a babysitter as her own sisters were too young to do it. She approached an older man in the neighbourhood and asked him if he would ask one of his daughters to mind us because she was going to her friend's party with my father. He told mam that one of his daughters would be more than happy to do it. Later that night when the babysitter arrived, she noticed that we did not speak in front of our father. We were like dummies in our chairs. We all knew if we opened our mouths in front of him, he would go on and on about it after the person had left. It was easier in the long run to keep our mouths shut. However, as soon as our father left for the night, we began to natter to the babysitter. During the night, some of my father's relations called in and started to complain to my mother. They said that my mother had insulted them in front of the babysitter. My mother called the babysitter and asked the young girl if my mother had made any comment about my father's family. The babysitter said my mother had said nothing about them. I was shocked to hear that the poor babysitter was dragged into the middle of this family squabble. It appeared to me that there was something wrong with all of them. I heard that the girl had been very upset over this matter. I could understand why she never returned to baby-sit us again.

There was a well down the hill that belonged to my great grandmother, where most of our neighbours would fetch water. However, my granddad stopped them from doing it. I remember on one occasion, a deaf and dumb lady came to fetch water from the well. My grandfather sarcastically shouted at her and called her names. He was trying to keep the well to himself. That's when I realised that my granddad was like my father.

Around the same time we were preparing to have the Stations of the Cross at home. Every year, people in our community had the Stations of the Cross in their homes. The mass would be read in the house and the rest of the family would gather around. Mam asked my father to be at home for the mass. He said that he had better things to do than stand around empowering a priest. At the end of the service, my father miraculously returned to partake of the food and alcohol. I had an enjoyable time with my neighbours at the stations that night. I remember the priest was a nice person. I enjoyed the mass. I was going around serving tea, sandwiches and biscuits. The first person I gave the sweet cake to was my schoolteacher. My uncle said that I was favouring the teacher hoping I would not get homework, but I genuinely liked her as she was always kind. She used to visit us every now and again whenever she had the chance. She used to bring a lot of magazines with her and she told mam that it would be very helpful for me to read them. She also used to bring lots of other stuff with her for me. On occasion, my mother used to send me to her house on errands. She used to tell me to spend a while at her house. However, I had to keep an eye on my watch as I knew that my father would give out to me if I spent more than 30 minutes away from home. I found it difficult visiting somebody's house when I was being timed as I had to rush home again.

A week after the Stations of the Cross had been performed in our home, I saw a shadow appearing and heard some noises outside my bedroom door. My brother was across from me and heard the noises on the kitchen floor himself. I didn't feel so bad as I wasn't the only one. He got out of bed and stared down at the back kitchen floor when he heard footsteps. When we told our family, my father turned around and said,

"Imagine that, only a week after mass has been read here. That shows you that mass is no good." Mam told him that the priest didn't speak to get rid of ghosts. My father reminded her that the priest had blessed the house and that should have been enough to cast out anything that was unholy. My father claimed that he had seen a ghost appear on the wall where the picture of Jesus was kept years earlier. He told me that the picture moved on occasion. When he told our parents exactly where he had heard the footsteps, my father told us that the old ladies used to say that nobody should build an extension from a house over a boithrin that goes down to a well. He told me the shadows could have appeared due to the fact that he had built an extension and blocked the boithrin to the well. He told my brother that the extension started from where he heard the footsteps. He spent days going on about it, wondering was it a result of that.

One day, I ran home from school knowing that my brothers and I had the house to ourselves. As soon as we got in the house my younger brother Niall found a letter on the table. 'Jesus,' he said'. When he realised that he couldn't sit around and watch television in peace after school. He was annoyed when he read the letter out loud to us. He said that our parents had asked him to bring in a few bags of turf for the night and wash the driveway and to bring out the ashes from the fire. He told me that my name was on the list and that our parents had given me a list of chores to do as well. I had to wash the dishes and mop the hall and the back kitchen and put the clothes out on the line, when they were ready. I hated all the work, especially having to wash the windows. This entailed bringing a chair and climbing on it. Niall told Tony that he did not have to do any work. He was the eldest and was supposed to look after us and report to our parents. Tony was no saint. He got the spare set of car keys, went outside and started up the blue Massey Ferguson tractor that my father had parked in front of the house. I went over to the tractor and told Tony that I couldn't reach the top of the window, that it was too high. I was upset and angry. I grabbed the bucket and threw the water on the window and it went all over the place. Niall got angry because he was given a job to clean the driveway and now he had to go back on it again. I left the window wet, knowing it would dry quickly as the sun was shining. I did the same job to every window in the house. We made sure we had everything done quickly before our parents returned. My brother reversed the tractor back and fourth in the garden, speeding about, delighted with himself but half-concerned that next door would inform on him. When our parents returned home later that afternoon, my father looked around the house to see if anything was out of place. He told Niall to lift the barrel of gas out of the back of the boot. I pulled the remainder of the shopping bags out with mam.

On another occasion, we came home to a similar note. I picked it up this time. It was quite similar to the last one. I had to wash out the fridge and mop the house. The work was given to Niall and I, excluding Tony again. At that time, my parents had two cars. Tony retrieved the keys from the jug and started driving the car and began reversing it back and fourth. He burnt up a lot of fuel because of this. My uncle saw him doing it and had a good laugh. However, he had a problem when the car got stuck on the hill. It took a while to place the car in its original position. On all occasions, one of us would act as lookout to ensure our parents didn't discover that we were driving one of the cars. We used to keep an eye on the road for our parents return.

Later that week, I overheard my uncle talking to a man about his car. However, the man realised that my uncle was not concentrating and had little interest in the conversation and merely played with the ring on his finger. John, the man my uncle had been working on the car for asked my father whether his brother ever received toys to play with when he was a child as he couldn't stop playing with a ring instead of listening to him. My father laughed and told the man that his brother didn't have many toys.

Later that afternoon, my father brought my sister and I into Spiddal. On our way, my father dropped into our local petrol station to get petrol. As ever, my father put five pounds worth of petrol in the car. As my father was paying for the petrol, the man asked him why he only ever put 5 pounds of petrol in the car. My father told him that he wasn't getting the petrol for nothing and that the man should keep his questions to himself. When my father returned to the car he told us to always check and make sure that no one took advantage of you

THROWING STONES

A week later, my mother was admitted to hospital. After a few days, mam returned from hospital and everybody enquired where she had been. My father told them that she had been at her uncle's in Galway when in fact, my mother had been admitted to Galway hospital due to my father beating her. It happened on two other occasions as well. When mam returned home, I told her that my father had made me wear the dungarees with holes in them to school. When she discovered that Niall wore the same shirt to school everyday without changing, she slapped him across the face.

One day, I heard my father shouting at his parents next door. There was only a small wall between our two houses. When I walked out, I saw my father shouting at his father. My father grabbed a rock. My grandfather shouted at him to throw it. My father threw the stone over the wall. Granddad jumped. It barely missed his feet. Later that day, my father's sister told my mother that my father had attempted to seduce her friend the previous night in her apartment. I looked at mam. She went pale and asked her to repeat the story. My uncle said something to his sister. My father's sister turned at him quickly and told him if he didn't shut his mouth that all the things that he had done would be brought out. I couldn't believe it. He looked so embarrassed.

At the time, the weather was quite cold. There was frost on the road and one of my friends slipped while we were playing in the school playground and cut her hand. My classmates and I ran over and lifted her to her feet. After school was finished, the girl contrived a story and told her mum that I had pushed her. When I reached home, my parents told me that the girl had complained about me pushing her. I started crying and told mam the truth. I said that there were three other girls who witnessed it. The following day, I questioned the girl regarding the incident. She blushed and walked away from me. I took a shortcut home in the afternoon from school with my other friend and I told her all about it. She laughed and made me feel better.

My father used to do a little bit of work every now and again on the bog. One day he dropped my brothers at the place where they were supposed to work and took me with him. I did not expect anything to happen to me in the car. He drove up to the lake and told me that he was going to tell me something about one of his family members. H told me that he had sold a car to one of his relatives a few days earlier and that his relative had set fire to the car the previous night as the police had been chasing him. My father alleged that the person had been exposing his private part to children in the park and that someone had witnessed the event and had telephoned the police and made complaints against him. I suspected in the beginning that it could have been my father himself who did it. Suddenly, I realised that there was more than one sick person from that bloodline. When he had finished telling the story he started the car and we drove off . Eventually, he drove off the main road down a by-lane and stopped at the end of the lane, looked everywhere to see if anyone was around. When he was satisfied that we were alone, he turned the ignition off and proceeded to rape me. As he raped me, I cried. It was extremely painful. I wondered how my father could inflict such pain on me. Had he forgotten that I had a soul. How could he hurt his own child? When he finished he tried to console me. But it didn't console me to hear that I was beautiful and that he no longer had any interest in my mother. He told me that I should never let any man come near me. On our way home, my father dropped into the shop at the bottom of our hill and bought me some liquorice sweets. As we drove up the hill he told me to cheer up and put a bright face on in front of my mother and siblings. There was no way I could act normally or pretend to be happy after this incident. A packet of sweets would not rectify the wrongdoing. I felt like I could explode with anger. When I joined my siblings in the sitting room, I told my brother the story my father had told me regarding the car. At the time, I felt that I could confide in my brother. However, he told the story back to my father. When my father learnt I told Tony, he hit me and told me that he would not be taking me to Dublin the following day. He spent time on his own chatting to Tony. I overheard him saying that I should never be trusted and that I was a dangerous liar.

The following morning, as my father prepared to travel to Dublin on the early train, my father repeated that I wouldn't be accompanying him to Dublin. He told me that he would be taking Tony with him instead. As he prepared to leave, he entered my bedroom and said "you're going to miss the trip because of your big mouth. When they left, I thought he and my brother were appropriate company for one another.

Several days after my father had returned from Dublin, my father put my brother Niall and I outside the house for the night. My father had made a wooden circle in the field and told mam that he was going to put us out in it as he hated having kids in the house. He ordered us out of the house and told us that we had to sleep outside in the wooden thing that he made in the centre of the garden. My mother pleaded with him to let us remain in the house. I recall looking at the stars that night. In the beginning, we were afraid of the dark. However, after a while we became accustomed to the dark and began to tune into all sorts of noises. Niall told me that it was more peaceful outside than it would be in the house listening to my father. We spent a while looking at the stars. Later that night, while my father was asleep, mam managed to bring us back into the house.

The following week, my uncle was rushed to Galway hospital having cut his head while fixing a car. When my mother visited him in hospital the following day, he told her that he was sick of his life and would have been happy if he had died. He had been unemployed for several years and the strain had taken its toll. Finding work in the west of Galway at that time was extremely difficult.

How To Avoid Paying Tv Licence

One night there was an interesting documentary on TV. There were characters in it speaking with a strong Dublin accent. It revolved around a father who had been sexually abusing his daughter. Mam called me from my bedroom and asked me to join the rest of the family and watch the documentary. Mam told my brothers that they should know that it was a programme about a man sexually abusing one of his daughters. She thought it would educate us and open our eyes about what goes on in the world. Our mother told us that this type of behaviour went on throughout the country but was seldom reported. My father was sitting on the small coffee table picking his nails nervously. He told my mother that she shouldn't be saying things like that to us. He started making movements on the table and whistling to distract mam from talking about the drama. I kept my head down at the time and found it all very upsetting.

A few days later, my father returned home from the bog early yelling as he came in the door that a TV licence inspector was in the locality checking to see if everybody had a TV licence. My father, of course, had forgotten to acquire aforementioned licence. As soon as my father entered the house, he went into the sitting room, disconnected the TV and carried it into his bedroom where he placed it into a wardrobe with a cushion over it. When he returned to the sitting room, he told us to go out in the garden and play and let him know as soon as any stranger approached the house. Shortly afterwards, Niall spotted a man in a suit walking up our hill. Niall turned and ran into the house. My sisters and I followed him. My mother was a little nervous and asked my father to go out to the gate and speak to the man. My father told my mother not to worry. Seconds later, the inspector walked in our gate. Before he reached the front door, my father stuck his head out the sitting room window, called the man over and asked him what he wanted. The man told my father that he was a TV inspector and was checking that households in the area had a current licence. My father told the inspector that we didn't have a TV. The inspector asked him how he managed without a Television? My father told him that people did without TV years ago. I laughed when I spotted the TV aerial sticking out of the wardrobe. My father told him that the last time he had a television was before he built the house. My father claimed that there was nothing good on it, anyway. When my father asked the inspector if he would like to come into the house and check, the inspector said that he believed my father and that there would be no need. My father laughed as the inspector strolled down the hill.

Another day, I was playing soccer with my brothers when the old man from our neighbourhood walked up towards our gate. We used to run up to him excitedly because he was always kind to us. As we chatted to the old man, a silver van pulled up outside our gate. A man rolled the window down and enquired about a certain house in the neighbourhood. We pointed out the house to him. He then asked if I would go with him and show him the house. Thank god the old man was standing there and heard everything. He intervened and said that it was not necessary at all and that he would break his stick across the man's back if he did not leave at once. When the van had left, the old man went into my mother and told her about the incident. She said that she had heard on the radio that kids were missing from the Clifden area, in North Galway. I was shaken by the incident and was so thankful for the old man's intervention. He was a very kind person as his entire family was. I never saw them fighting or arguing. I remember Tony tried a few puff s of his pipe and got sick afterwards. The old man started laughing and told Tony that was the best thing that could have happened to him and that it would put him off cigarettes for life. He was right. He enjoyed telling us interesting stories. I learned a lot from him. He came up with wonderful sayings like "its always a new broom that sweeps clean first'. We never tired of his company. Some days, I knew the elderly man was in the sitting room as I could smell his pipe smoke as soon as I entered the house. I liked the smell of the pipe. I laughed when I heard him say "a fly would never enter a sealed mouth".

At the time, my brother Niall and I had developed a new pastime. We would roll a barrel to the top of a hill and one of us would jump into the barrel. The other would roll the barrel to the bottom of the hill. We had great fun.

Weeks later, my father entered my bedroom. It was obvious that he had been drinking. He looked out the window and then looked back at the bed where I was sleeping. He approached my bed and sat on it. He started to speak. His words were a little slurred. I pretended to be asleep. He started to nudge me. I still pretended to be asleep. He then started to shaking me. I woke immediately. He started to pull back the blankets on my bed. I felt cold. As he revealed my nightclothes, he placed his hand on my stomach. I felt extremely uncomfortable. He started to run his hand over my body, and began to lift up my nightdress. Suddenly, footsteps could be heard outside my bedroom door. He immediately stood up, throwing the blankets over me in the process. As he walked towards the window, my mother entered my bedroom. She looked at me and then looked at my father. She immediately asked him what he was doing in my bedroom at that hour of the night. He said that he thought he had heard noises outside and was worried that someone might be looking through the window at me. Mam thought something was wrong. She approached my bed, pulled up the quilt and looked at my blue nightdress. I looked at her sadly as I pulled down my nightdress as it was half way up. Mam looked at the nightdress and a look of uncertainty crossed her eyes. She gave my father a strange look. My father became embarrassed. He was trembling. She told him that he was keeping me awake and to go back to bed. After a couple of minutes, I heard my parents arguing in their bedroom. I heard my father slapping my mother and asking her 'what did you think was going on?' The following morning, I was too tired to get up for school as I had been up most of the night. It had been around 4.30am before I got to sleep. When I finally awoke, I spent half the day sitting on my bed looking through my window. I was tearful and found it difficult to concentrate on anything.

Days later, my father called me into the shed. While the rest of the family were in the house, he raped me. When he was finished, he told me that he would be unable to have me to himself as my mother had become a little suspicious and was keeping a close eye on him. As I was dressing, my father spotted my mother approaching the shed. He told me to hurry. My mother entered the shed and asked my father what he was doing. He told her that he had been fixing some tools. As she turned to leave, she called me and asked me to help her in the house.

I have a few fond memories of my final year in sixth class National School. My brother and I decided to join a summer camp. As always, it was difficult for us to get permission to go to the camp. Eventually my father relented. My father instructed my brother to keep a close eye on me. On the bus to the camp, we all sang. There were 4 boys from my class on the bus. On our first day at the camp, we learned how to play basketball and also participated in art classes and learned how to make little puppets. We had a different tutor for each activity. Two of our tutors were from my mother's village and were very kind to us. Our parents had given us money for the two nights. I was happy to be away from my father. That afternoon, we went up Croagh Patrick. I found it difficult to climb. When we reached the Summit of Croagh Patrick, some of the group entered the little church and took confession. When the last person was finished in confession, we began the descent. I found it much easier on the way down and managed not to fall once. That night, I shared a tent with two other girls. I slept well the first night but the second night the weather worsened and our tent was damaged. We ran over to where the tutors were sleeping and told them that our tent was damaged. One of the tutors returned with us and fixed the tent in a matter of minutes.

When I awoke the following morning, I felt sad that I couldn't remain at the camp. I had thoroughly enjoyed my experience with the group. The tutors had been very helpful. There was one particular boy who had a lovely face that I was going to miss. I hoped that some one like him would someday deliver me from my miserable life. I felt very broken going home. My younger brother was as upset as I was. On our way home on the bus, we sang. When we arrived home, one of the tutors told us that we were all going to be invited to a party in two weeks time. I was happy when I learned that I was going to see that nice boy's face again. Our parents welcomed us when we returned and asked us about the camp.

Two weeks later my mother received a letter with an invitation for us to attend the party. Thankfully we were allowed to go. They played good songs from the 70's and 80's. I noticed the boy from the summer camp looking in my direction. I was hoping he would ask me up for a slow dance, but sadly he never did. Perhaps he was too shy. I watched him walking in and out of the club. The boy lived next door to my other granny in Lettermore. He used to visit my uncle all the time. He knew I visited my granny every now and again. I felt sad when the party was over as I didn't get the chance to talk to him. Whenever my brother mentioned his name, my eyes always lit up. I thought about my uncle in Lettermore and felt my uncle was privileged to be this young boy's friend.

I will never forget the day my elder brother Tony and I spotted our father opening his accordion with a screwdriver. When he opened the accordion, bundles of notes fell to the ground. He lifted them off the floor and began counting them. He looked at ease counting the notes. When we approached our father and asked him where he had got the money, he told us that he had stolen the money from one of our neighbours. He told us that people had no faith in banks and had a habit of stashing money somewhere in their houses. When we asked him if he was afraid of being caught, he told us that the police weren't clever enough to open the accordion and that they'd never know where the money was stashed.

Two weeks later, my father told me that he had robbed another one of our neighbours. When I asked him how he had managed to do it a second time, he told me that he had stolen the money from some elderly people who lived near us while they attended mass in the National School. He told me that one of his family members had helped him. He told me that when they entered the house at first that they couldn't find any money and began to lose hope. He told me that he then decided to search the attic. When he climbed into the attic he found a biscuit box that contained the money. He turned it upside down and a bundle of money fell out. He mentioned that he was supposed to share the money with his accomplice.

However, he decided to pocket most of the money for himself. When he came down from the attic, he had a few of the notes in his hand. He told his accomplice that was all he had found. They shared the money and left the premises. When he told me what he had done I felt disgusted at him and wondered why he couldn't be like a normal father and work for a living.

Once my father bought a cow with an unusual coco colour. We called it Shirley. He would always send my brother down the fields to feed her potato skins. He would seldom go down himself. One day, as my brothers and I walked home from school, a lady from the local shop approached us and asked us if we were the owners of the cow that was standing in the middle of the road. We looked down the road and spotted Shirley ambling along. Niall, who absolutely adored the cow, dropped his school bag on the ground and ran towards Shirley. When he reached Shirley, he patted her on the shoulder. He then led her up the road towards our house. When he had managed to lead her into our garden he started to play with her.

Another day, while my mother was visiting her family member, my father brought me out to a field and raped me in view of his mother's house. When I reached home, I went straight to my brothers' room. They asked me where I had been and told me that I had missed the best part of the film. I could not sit in the room. I felt miserable. I went to my bedroom and slept. A little later, my father came up and asked me to wash my face and cheer up. I didn't want to get up. I felt restless and lethargic. Everything was getting on top of me. As he left my room, he warned me to have a smile on my face when I got out of bed.

That evening, when my mother returned, she told me to take the clothes off the line. As I was taking the clothes off the line, I spotted my uncle removing a window frame from his sister's mobile home that was parked across from Granny's house. He then got in the window and began making noises as if he was searching for something. My father was standing at the wall watching him. I knew that my father was somehow involved. A few minutes later, my uncle emerged from the mobile home. He then replaced the window and started to walk towards my father. When I had taken the clothes off the line, I walked slowly towards the house hoping to overhear what my father and my uncle were saying. I heard my uncle telling my father that his brother-in-law was stupid and all that he had in the house were antidepressants and prescriptions. He commented that it wasn't a wonder that his sister's husband didn't have a job and that he spent most of his time running to the Doctors' surgery. My father told his brother that he hated the man because he always went on about having a black belt in Karate. That comment annoyed my father.

The following Sunday afternoon, my father challenged him in the local pub. My father claimed that he grabbed the man by the neck in the toilet. When a total stranger saw my father pulling out a pocket-knife he ran out of the toilet. My father threatened to kill him and told him that if he mentioned the black belt again that he would stab him. When our father returned from the pub that afternoon, he told us what had happened. My mother asked my father why he had challenged his brother-in-law. My father said that his sister had married a waster and that he needed to be taken down a peg. An hour later, a police car pulled up outside the house. Three police officers emerged from the car and approached the front door. My father opened the door and went out and spoke to the police officers in the back of the police car. My father told the police officers that the man was lying and was on various medications and also had a criminal record. I was hoping that my father would be arrested and sent to jail. As soon as he came in the door, he told my mother that everything was fine and that no policeman in the world would listen to the man next door.

One Saturday evening, when my father returned from the pub, he told us that he had dropped into one of the neighbour's gardens on the way home and had taken some of their underwear off their clothes line and put it on one of their donkeys. He thought it was extremely funny. The following morning, when the minibus arrived to collect the elderly ladies for mass, my next door neighbour who was on the bus, told my mother that all the people on the bus were roaring laughing when they spotted a bra on the elderly ladies donkey. The two elderly ladies who recognised their underclothes were extremely embarrassed and asked how anybody could be so wicked as to put their underclothes on a poor animal. All the people on the bus couldn't stop laughing all the way to mass. The entire conversation on the bus to mass was about who would be so wicked as to take the elderly ladies underwear and place it on the donkey. My mother merely looked at our neighbour and said nothing.

Whenever my father was bored, he sat in his car and spun the tyres of the car hoping that someone would come out of the house and pay him some attention. Mam used to say, "What the hell has gone into him?" He used to spin the chips and speed down the road. My brothers and I rushed out to the wall and watched him speeding down the road.

At that time, Niall and I were planning to run away from home. As we discussed our plans and tried to figure out who would go out the window first that night, we noticed that Tony was listening to our conversation. Later that evening, Tony told our parents what we were planning to do. Our plans had been foiled. From that moment on, we were watched like hawks.

1990/1991 LOCAL HALL OPENED

When the Hall opened in Camas, our school arranged to have a social night. In class we practised reciting poetry and telling stories. The school arranged for a band to play when all the readings were finished. When the night arrived, my mother who had been in Rosmuc for the day returned home sporting a black eye. We all knew that our father had given her the black eye. She told me that she was waiting for my father to return with the car so she could bring my brothers and I to the function. While we waited for our father, we rehearsed the pieces we had learned for the show. As the clock approached 8.00pm, my father still hadn't arrived. My mother looked concerned but there was nothing she could do. Eventually, we heard the car approaching. When my father entered the house, my mother merely asked him for the car keys. The atmosphere in the house was quite intense. My father handed her the keys. My mother told us to collect everything we needed and jump in the car. When we arrived at the hall, everyone noticed my mother's black eye. The word quickly went round that my father had struck her. When we were called on stage, my brother and I recited a poem. There was a man at the front of the stage using a camera. As we recited the poem, I began to smile when I spotted Fr. Keane in the front of the audience. Fr Keane smiled back at me. Fr. Keane's smile encouraged me. After I had recited the poem with my brother, I then sang a song. At first, I felt very nervous. However, after a few lines, I began to improve. My brother told me later that he was surprised that I had such courage and was easily able to stand in front of a camera and sing at the top of my voice. I thoroughly enjoyed the night, especially the singing. I always had a passion for music. I couldn't go a day without listening to music. As a child, music consoled me. I felt it was the best therapy for my mind. I wrote songs in a little red notebook that I had. I then sang the songs and taped them onto a blank tape. Whenever I mentioned to my family that I wanted to be a singer when I grew up, they told me that I didn't have the talent and that it was impossible to make a living out of singing. As ever, my family were very supportive.

One weekend, my mother bought me into Galway city and bought me a lovely long red jacket. She told me that I needed it as I would be starting secondary school after the summer. When my mother and I returned from Galway city, my brother Niall was not happy to see me sporting a new jacket. He asked my mother why she was always buying me new clothes and why he never got anything new. He continued complaining to her about the matter all day. When my mother began to ignore his whining, he went to my father and started to complain. My father checked my wardrobe and told my mother that she was buying me too many new clothes. I knew that Niall had sparked my father. My father told my mother that the same clothes should have done me for another while. Niall's mood changed when he heard my father complaining to my mother about the new red jacket I had received. My mother told my father that I needed a jacket with a hood on it as I was starting secondary school in a few weeks time. One day as my father and I walked down the road towards the local shop, my father spotted a man in the distance walking towards us. My father told me that the man had been a patient in the psychiatric ward in Galway Hospital. He then told me that if that man ever committed a crime that he wouldn't be prosecuted as he could claim that he was mentally unstable and unaware of what he was doing. He told me that anybody who attended a psychiatric ward was classed as not being the full shilling. When my father realised that the man was heading towards the shop, he grabbed me by the arm and turned and walked back towards our home. He told me that it was better not to have any contact with mental patients. I looked back at the man and wondered what wrong he had ever done on my father.

Patrick Naughton, P.I.

Towards the end of the summer, my father bought a curragh. He brought the wooden boat home as it needed some repairs. When he finally repaired the curragh, he placed it on top of our car and drove to the "cave", a place where people moored their boats and left the boat there. When he returned home, he told my mother that he intended to go fishing in the curragh the following day. When he drove back to the cave the following morning the boat was nowhere to be seen. He began to search for the missing boat. When he reached the little bridge, he noticed that the green van that belonged to some lodgers who were staying with one of our neighbours had been pushed into the little river. He initially thought that an accident had taken place and went down to investigate. When he approached the van he spotted his boat submerged under the van. When he returned home, he dropped over to our neighbour's house and telephoned the police. When the police arrived on the scene, he asked them how long it would take them to find out who had destroyed his boat. They told him they would do everything that they could do but were unable to give him a specific timeframe. He told the police that there were particular people he suspected of committing this crime. He then gave the police the names of the people he suspected. He told them that he was sure that his own brother was somehow involved. As soon as the police left, he cursed them and said that he would personally take charge of his own investigation and that he would handle the matter without any police assistance. My mother told him to wait and see if the police found out who was involved. He shouted at her and started mocking the police "I will find out quicker myself..... I will carry out my own investigation and leave no stone unturned. They will only go easy on people when they question them. But watch what I'll do". He called out the names of his primary suspects. He told my mother that he had a plan. He told her that he would question one of the people he suspected. He said that he would tell the person that the other people who were involved had confessed and that there was no point in denying their involvement. My mother told him that he shouldn't be accusing anyone. He said that he would bring Tony along as a witness. My father and Tony then drove off in the car. As soon as my father spotted the miscreant, he called him over. The miscreant sounded nervous when my father questioned him. The man denied any involvement, but my father told him that he would stop him from going to college in future if he didn't admit to his involvement and give the names of the others who were involved. The man continued to deny having any involvement. My father decided to question another man and extract the truth from him. My father was bent on catching the young man before anyone else spoke to him. He drove like a lunatic and spotted the man standing at a shed. My father whistled at him and beckoned him to come over. My father said "The rest of the lads have admitted their guilt and have agreed to pay the price of the boat." The young lad blushed. He didn't know what to say. My father asked him if he was prepared to pay his part of the damages. The young man nodded and said that he would pay his part of the damages. My father smiled immediately. The young man explained to my father that it was an accident and that they hadn't realised that my father's boat was in the cave when they pushed the van over the bridge. The young man innocently told my father the names of all the people involved. Before my father left, he told the young man that if he did not want his name to be splashed in the papers that he should pay the damages as quickly as possible. The man replied that he would pay his share of the damages as quickly as he could and tell the others to do the same. He was very apologetic about the whole episode. My father said that the matter would be resolved as soon as the damages were paid. My father was very excited and rushed to another man's house before anybody had a chance to talk to him. When my father reached the man's home, he told him that he knew exactly what had happened and who was involved. My father related the whole story and the young man was surprised to hear how accurate my father's retelling was. He told the man that he wanted the damages paid as quickly as possible. The man apologised and said that he would pay his part of the damages as soon as he had the money. When my father returned home, he triumphantly related his exploits to my mother and told her how he had single-handedly resolved the matter. He said that the damages for the boat would be paid very quickly.

The following morning, as my mother listened to the local news on the radio, she heard that a lady she knew very well from our village was very ill. She turned to my father and said that she would have to listen in case the woman passed away. My father asked her why she would spend the day listening to a radio waiting for someone to die and why people in the area were fascinated with other people's misery. My mother said that she knew the woman very well and was hoping that the woman would recover. My father asked her why she cared ether the woman lived or not. He said "Jesus Christ, that's their problem not yours. If she dies so what. Her time was up. What's the big deal? She's old. It's time she passed on. She would only be taking up space for the new generation. What's the big fuss? She had enough time spent here, Jesus it would be worse if a young person was dying. An old person, Jesus, that's to be expected." As I listened, I realised that he lacked any emotion for his fellow human beings.

The following morning, my mother awoke and started to mop the floor. When I entered the sitting room, my father was lying on the sofa, watching my mother working. This was a skill he had developed over the years. When my mother had finished mopping the floor, she looked at my father and said "Jesus, you will sleep your life away." My mother told my father that she was bored and wanted my father to take her for a drive. He immediately lost the head and told her to get lost and that he wanted some peace and quiet. He asked her what did she mean "bored" and told her that she was starting to sound like the children. Moments later, my mother disappeared into one of the bedrooms. The front door opened and Niall entered and proceeded to drag his mucky boots across the clean floor. A few minutes later, mam returned and asked me who had dirtied the floor. I told her that Niall had come in from the garden and had walked on the floor. She started complaining that she had spent the entire morning washing the floor. She called Niall from his bedroom.. When he entered the sitting room, my mother asked him why he had muddied her clean floor. He told her that our father had asked him to bring in a bag of turf from the back garden. My mother began to remop the sitting floor. As she mopped, my father commented on a holy picture we had hanging from one of the walls. My father called all of us into the sitting room and told us to look at the holy picture of Jesus on the wall. As we looked at the holy picture, our father said that the eyes of Jesus moved when the sun shone on them. He said the picture was haunted. He told my mother that all the Holy pictures in the house should be taken down and thrown out. He said that the pictures brought nothing but bad luck. My mother looked at him in shock and told him not to be saying such things in front of the children and not to be turning the children against the church. She said it was small wonder that Tony never listened to the priest when he was at mass. My father smiled and said that he was glad that Tony ignored the priest. My father told my mother that Tony had a mind of his own and would decide himself if there was anything "above" him. My father said to my mother, "Surely if a child can work out it's all bullshit, the rest of the people out there should know it's all fake......priests, they're all fakers......I told you before, it's all bullshit.....you go there every Sunday, for what?......and why do the priests encourage women to have more children when they already have too many.....well........" My mother looked at my father and left the room. When my mother returned into the sitting room, she asked my father to drive my two sisters to the crossroads where a minibus collected them and brought them to Oughterard for swimming lessons. I asked my mother if I could go with them. My mother nodded. I was delighted to be out of the house.

Later that week, a funny incident occurred. Two ladies from our neighbourhood asked my father if he would drive them to Carraroe to do some shopping. The ladies said they would pay him for his time. My father agreed. When they arrived in Carraroe, the two ladies headed off to do their shopping. My father left my sister and I in the back seat of the car and headed towards the pub. When our father entered the pub, we jumped out of the car and walked around the town as we knew our father would be in no rush to leave the pub. When we returned to the car an hour later, the two elderly ladies were sitting in the back of the car. When we opened the car door to get in, the two ladies asked us where our father was. We told the ladies that our father was in the pub. The ladies asked us to drop into the pub and ask our father how long he would be. We dropped into the pub and spotted our father sitting on a bar stool chatting to an elderly man. We approached him and told him that the two ladies had returned to the car and were wondering when he'd be ready to leave. He told us to tell them that he would be out in five minutes. We returned to the car and told the ladies what our father had said. We then waited. An hour passed and my father had not yet appeared. The ladies asked us to drop into the pub again and see what was keeping our father. When we entered the pub and told our father that the ladies were complaining, he decided to return to the car with us. When we reached the car, the ladies asked him why he had left them waiting in the car for the past two hours. He shouted back "nobody fuckin asked ye to wait. Why didn't ye make your own way home. All ye women are the same, not happy unless ye are complaining and gossiping". The elderly women looked up at him in shock. He told them to get their arses out of the car and to make their own way home. He told them that it would teach them a lesson and that maybe in future they wouldn't be complaining all the time. When the ladies left, my father brought the two of us back into the pub.

The following week, my brothers and I spotted our grandfather bailing hay in a field across from his house. Our grandfather was a rather taciturn character at the best of times. Whenever a neighbour visited him, he would either ignore them completely, begin reading a newspaper or higher the volume on the television. By this stage, he had managed to alienate himself from every one of his neighbours in the locality. When my aunt, who was only a year older than me, spotted my brother and I sitting on the wall, she walked over and began chatting with us. As we chatted, we watched our grandfather bailing the hay. When he was finished he returned to his house. As soon as we spotted him entering his house, we decided to play a game of hide-and-seek in the same field.

We entered the field and began rolling around in the hay. We were having a wonderful time until our grandfather spotted us. He emerged from the house and began screaming at us. We all scattered. He chased after us and caught my aunt. He slapped her across the face and her glasses fell to the ground. My brothers and I felt sorry for our aunt as she wiped the tears from her eyes. He then told her to return to the house. My brothers and I jumped over the wall and returned home.

A few weeks later, my mother decided to bring all of us to Knock. My father was not too keen on the idea, but eventually relented. It was a beautiful day when we arrived in Knock. There were lots of stalls selling crosses, religious pictures and religious ornaments. My mother bought crosses for all of us. My father approached one stall and began speaking to an elderly woman. After a couple of moments, I spotted my father praying. At the time, I found the episode very confusing and wondered how my father could constantly criticise the church on the one hand and then pray on the other. On the way home from Knock, we listened to tapes of Philomena Begley and Susan McCann that my father had in the car. My father always said that they were the only good Country-and-Western singers that could sing.

Two weeks later, we received word that my father's cousin in Toureen had died. My father asked me to attend the funeral with him. Initially, we drove to Spiddal where my father met his uncle Paddy in one of the local pubs. Paddy told my father that he hated funerals and was dreading the thought of going to the house for the removal. My father told him not to worry and that it would be all over in a few hours. When we left the pub, we headed towards Toureen. When we arrived at the house, the remains of my father's uncle were lying in the front room. I recognised several of my father's family. Suddenly, my father spotted one of his brothers who approached us. My father began chatting to his brother. His brother mentioned that it was now possible to bring a dead man back to life. My father looked startled and asked his brother not to be making such comments. When his brother continued in this vein, my father tried to change the topic of conversation, but to no avail. His brother told him that it was possible to place plastic rods in the deceased man's sides to bring him back to life. He then told the people around him to take the miserable looks off their faces as it was possible to bring the dead man back to life. My father blushed with embarrassment and tried to make light of his brother's comments. My father looked at his brother and told him not to be making such comments as it would disturb the deceased man's wife. However, his brother was not for stopping and started roaring laughing. His brother turned around and said "well, she should be glad to hear that somebody has come up with an interesting idea on how to bring her husband back to life". He then started to talk about an operation he had seen on television where Doctors had placed iron cables on a patient's chest and had managed to bring the person back to life. Suddenly, he said that he could see the deceased man's chest moving up and down. All the people around the coffin stared at the dead man. My father's brother told the people around the coffin that the man was probably asleep and not dead at all and that the doctors had made a terrible mistake. Several people in the room began to laugh. At this stage, my father realised that there was no way of stopping his brother. My father walked over to the deceased man's wife and paid his respects. He looked back at me and gestured for me to follow him out the front door. When I returned home, I told my mother how funny one of my relative's was at the funeral. She had her hand over her mouth with embarrassment while I described his behaviour.

The following week, a young boy approached my younger brother Niall in school and asked him. "Does your father think that everybody is thick." My brother Niall looked at him quizzically and asked him what he was talking about. The young boy told Niall that my father wore a wig and that whenever there was a strong breeze that the wig would fly off my father's head and that the young boy had spotted my father chasing the wig along the road one day. My brother got embarrassed and told him to mind his own business. That afternoon, Niall rushed home from school. He barely had the chance to take a deep breath when he came in the door and told my father what the young boy had said. My father lost the head immediately, looked in the mirror and asked my mother "Does this look straight on my head. Does it look like a wig?" My mother told him that it looked like a wig and that she wouldn't be seen dead wearing a wig. He started kicking things and shouted "I paid 300 fucking pounds for this. I was told that it suits me. That little runt must have overheard his parents gossiping." Several days later, my mother told my father that she had seen a commercial on the television for REGAIN, a new product coming on the market that helped hair grow back and that she had also taken down the free phone number in case he wanted to give them a call. My father phoned them immediately and ordered some sprays. A week later, two bottles arrived in the post. He sprayed it on his scalp and after a couple of weeks his scalp turned brown to match the few strands of hair he still had on the side of his head. It looked a little odd. He decided to start wearing a green cap with holes in it. He believed that the holes would allow air to circulate around his scalp and encourage hair growth. Over a period of time, he used all sorts of home remedies, such as soaking his head in a bath full of freshly picked nettles or even seaweed to try and get his hair to grow back. The bath was always black after he had boiled nettles or seaweed in it.

My Confirmation

As we entered the Summer, school was ending and I was preparing for my confirmation that was to take place at the end of June. I asked my mother if we could go to Galway city and select a dress. She told me that she hadn't much money and that one of her sisters in England had already sent her a lovely dress in the post. She showed me the picture of a young girl wearing the dress. The dress was navy blue with polka dots. A couple of days before the confirmation, I still hadn't settled on the two names I was going to choose when being confirmed by the bishop. I spoke to my granny and mother but still couldn't decide. On the day of my confirmation, I rose early. As soon as I was dressed, I headed towards the kitchen for breakfast. As had happened at my Communion, my father said that he wouldn't be standing with me at the altar. My mother looked at my father in dismay and tried to persuade him to change his mind, but he was not to be swayed. My mother dropped into my Granny's house next door and asked my godfather if he would stand for me at the confirmation. After breakfast, my cousin, who was a hairdresser, arrived at the house. As she was styling my hair, she told my father to stop cutting my hair and to let my curls grow. When 3 o'clock arrived, we headed off for the church. When we arrived at the church, I spotted a boy from my class who was also being confirmed and my headmaster. My headmaster walked over to me and told me that I looked beautiful in my dress. During the Mass, my headmaster sat next to me. Another teacher from my school was busy arranging the choir. When I looked in the choir's direction, I longed to join them. Halfway through the Mass, I turned my head and spotted my father standing at the back of the church. I was surprised to see him. I nudged my brother Tony and told him that my father was actually in the church. He looked at me in disbelief but changed his expression when he looked back and saw my father. I turned to my mother and told her that my father was actually in the church. She looked back, saw him and smiled. Towards the end of the Mass, the bishop called all the children who were to be confirmed to the altar. I rushed up and took my place on the altar, my mother and godfather at my side. Bishop Eamon Casey confirmed me. On my way back to my seat, I noticed that my father was nowhere to be seen. When we left the church, my aunt took lots of photos of me outside the church. My mother called my father over and asked him to stand beside me while my aunt took some photos. Eventually, my father joined me. When he put his arm around me, I felt sick. At this stage, my father's touch repulsed me. I couldn't wait for my aunt to finish taking the photos. When she finished, we headed home. Later that night, my whole family dropped down to the local pub where a band played music all night long.

A couple of weeks after my Confirmation, my father received a call from the secretary in the National School asking my father if he would be interested in painting some of the classrooms and fitting some new widows in the National school. As it was paid work, my father jumped at the chance. On the first morning that my father started painting the school, he asked my mother to send me down to the school with his lunch at lunchtime. He told her that I was constantly complaining about being bored and that the walk would do me the world of good. When my mother had made his sandwiches at lunchtime, she gave them to me and told me to drop them down to him at the school. On my way to the school, I spotted a stray dog on the side on the road. His eyes looked sad and delicate. It reminded me of how I felt. I gave the poor animal a couple of my father's sandwiches. When I arrived at the school, my father was painting a ceiling. I called him, placed his lunch on a table and turned to go as I wanted to be away from him as quickly as I could. He called me and told me to wait. He said that he hadn't spoken to a soul all day, other than the old man from the shop. When he approached me, his mood changed. He began cursing and said "Where is the fucking flask? Does she think I'm a fucking monkey and can eat sandwiches without a drink?" I was afraid. He then asked me if I had eaten some of the sandwiches on the way to the school. I didn't know what to say. As his ranting continued, I became more frightened. He told me to undress and lean on the table. I refused. He grabbed hold of me and started undressing me. He then placed his arms around my body and raped me. I found it difficult to breathe. When he was finished, he told me to dress. He then told me stories and tried to cheer me up. A few minutes later, the door opened and the old man from the shop entered. My father looked at him nervously. My father told the old man that he was having his lunch and to drop back later for a chat. The old man left. When the old man had gone, my father told me to put a smile on my face before returning home. When I reached home, I went straight into my bedroom and stared out of my window at the trees and clouds. For the remainder of the afternoon, I listened to the birds singing outside. I wondered why my father was hurting me? What had I done? What could I do to make him stop hurting me?

During that Summer, I became a big Tina Turner. She had a wonderful voice and was a very powerful singer. As an adult, I discovered that she had had a difficult marriage and had suffered physical abuse. Her music consoled me during a difficult period of my life.

SECONDARY SCHOOL

When September arrived, I started secondary school. A week before I started in secondary school, my father cut my hair so short that I looked like a boy. I was extremely self-conscious of my appearance and very sensitive about any negative comments at that time. One afternoon, when I returned home from school, I told my brothers that I had learned how to make queen cakes in school and would bake some queen cakes for them that evening. While I was baking, my father returned home, entered the kitchen and asked me to follow him down the road on my bike. I had no choice but to follow him. When I left the house, I grabbed my bike and followed my father. When I arrived at the top of the hill, just a few yards away from my home, I decided enough was enough. I decided I was going to end my life. I raced the bike down the hill as fast as I could, knowing I wouldn't be able to stop the bike. I heard my father's voice in the background calling after me. When I reached the road at high speed, there were sadly no cars passing. I crossed the road, crashed into a small wall and was thrown over the handlebars of the bike. When I hit the ground, I could feel pain all over. A couple of girls from our neighbourhood ran over to me to see if I was hurt.

Then, the old lady from the shop came over and told me that she would ring for an ambulance. Then my father arrived on the scene. He told the girls and the old woman not to worry and that he would look after everything. He lifted me off the ground and carried me to my old school. When we arrived at the school, he carried me into one of the sheds and raped me. The pain was excruciating. When he was finished, he told me to tell my mother that I had only scratched myself. When we returned home, my father placed a bandage on my hand. He then grabbed a stick and attached it along my arm with a blue roll. He told me the stick would help keep the bone straight until the following morning. My mother, who had been visiting a neighbour's house, arrived an hour later and asked me what had happened to my arm. My mother asked my father to bring me to casualty to have my arm x-rayed as I was complaining of the pain. My father told her that he'd wait until the following morning and that if my condition hadn't improved that he would take me to casualty. The following morning, my hand had swollen. I told my mother that I was unable to move my hand without causing myself severe pain. My mother told my father to take me to casualty directly. When the doctor examined my hand, he told my father that I had chipped a bone in my wrist and that my hand would have to be in a cast for several weeks. He also told my father that I needed a couple of months rest and shouldn't be asked to do anything physically demanding around the house.

When I returned home, I spent the following few days in bed with a cast on my right hand reading magazines. I was right handed and I couldn't go to school. I spent most of the following days chatting to my uncle who lived next door to us. Around the same time, my father told me that it wouldn't make any difference if I quit school just like he did at my age. He reminded me of his brother who had quit school at 14 and who now had his own successful business in England. One morning, I received a letter from one of my classmates.

She was concerned that I hadn't been in school for a couple of weeks. I wrote back to her and outlined in my letter that I had broken my wrist and could only write with my left hand. As I sat in the garden, reading my letter, my father appeared and asked me what I was doing. I told him that I was reading a letter I had received from one of my school friends. When he asked to look at the letter, I stood up and told him that it was nothing that he hadn't already read, as my letter had been opened before I received it.

Later that week, my father received a call from the secretary of the National School asking him to put in some new windows. The secretary told him that someone had broken the windows again and that this was sadly becoming a regular occurrence. When my father received the news, he turned to my mother, told her he had great news and smiled. When my father dropped down to the school the following morning, our local priest greeted him. My father never collected the wages for the work he did. He sent Niall to the lady in the committee to get it.

In the middle of November, I returned to school. I found it hard because there was so much to learn and the teacher was very strict. I was afraid of one of the teachers I had in secondary school. He used to speak very quickly in English and I found it difficult to follow him. At the time, I was under stress from my father at home and two boys in my class who ridiculed me all the time and called me dogface. They used to bark like a dog in the class. My brother told my father about the young boys. As soon as my father found out there were two bullies in my class, he found out their background history. He used to say to mam "That's why she is sad. Those low class tramps in school bullying her. It's too much for her to take. They're all jealous of her."

After Christmas, I was moved to a different classroom. My favourite teacher was a nun who taught me French and Religion. When the nun gave out the result of the French exams she said that everyone had failed other than me. One afternoon, the nun told me to tell my parents that she would be dropping around to my house later in the week to discuss with my parents how I was progressing in school. The following Saturday morning, she called round to our house. Mam met her at the gate and told her that I had mentioned that she would be dropping around to discuss my progress in school. Mam asked her into the house. As they were chatting, I made the tea. At first she started discussing my elder brother Tony and how well he had been getting on in second year. She told mam that he was able to concentrate well and picked things up easily. She mentioned that when she spoke to me about something in class that I seemed to have difficulties concentrating and that my mind appeared to be elsewhere. Mam asked me to join them in the living room.

The nun repeated the same question to me about the amount of time I spent looking out the window. She asked me was there something bothering me. I didn't know what to say. She told me that it must be something very bad due to the way I reacted. She looked at me and mam stared at the carpet. I told her there was something bothering me but I didn't know how to say it. She looked at my mother and told her that it must have been something bad the way I looked sad all the time. My mother told her that she didn't really know anything about it either. The teacher told her that she noticed me going out of the classroom and getting sick a lot. She said that it wasn't normal for a young girl. She told mam that it appeared that something had been distracting me from my school work and that I was unable to concentrate for any period of time. She left shortly afterwards. Later that evening when my father returned home, my mother told my father that one of my teachers had dropped around. My father told my mother that I was having trouble with some bullies in school. The matter was closed.

As the year progressed, the abuse continued. When I finished my First Year Summer exams in school, it was time for my brothers and I to return to the bog and help our father gathering turf. Our father would generally cut the turf from the ground. My brothers and I would then lift two pieces of turf and stand them against each other to help them dry out. As my health was quite weak at this time, I found it very difficult to work for more than a couple of hours. However, my father told me that if I didn't remain on the bog until they were finished, that he wouldn't let me sit beside the fire when the Winter came. One afternoon, my father and I were working on the bog alone. My father asked me if I understood the word rape. Before I replied, he began to relate certain incidents of rape he had read about in the newspapers. He told me that rape was when a man forced a woman to have sex with him at knifepoint. Quite often, the man would cut the clothes from the woman's body with a knife, my father told me. When he was finished explaining the word rape to me, he told me that he was going to continue using me as he had been doing. Again he threatened to hurt me if I told anybody. When we returned to the house that evening, I went straight to my bedroom and cried. I realised that my father had no intention of stopping. For the following three months, my two brothers and I worked on the bog cutting and storing turf with my father. As the Summer ended, I prepared to return to school to start second year. I was now 14 years old.

When I returned to school, I was obliged to participate in various sports. At this time, I was very conscious of my appearance. The abuse was beginning to affect my ability to communicate with my classmates. I was slowly becoming an introvert. One day, my cousin asked me if I would like to join his soccer team. Initially, I declined. However, my cousin was adamant and eventually convinced me to join. Our team was very successful and managed to win various school trophies during the year. This provided me with an opportunity to block out what was happening at home.

Christmas came and went. After Christmas when I returned to school, I realised that it was possible to become involved in music classes. I began to play the keyboard. During these classes, I began to develop a sincere interest in music. One of the boys from the neighbourhood who attended these classes played the guitar. I thoroughly enjoyed listening to him as he was an excellent guitarist. He enjoyed playing Garth Brooks songs. After several weeks, I was able to play a couple of songs. Our teacher took a keen interest in our development and constantly encouraged us. At the time, I wondered why my father couldn't be more like my music teacher.

One afternoon, after finishing a music class, I met my two brothers in the school yard. As we walked home, I told my brothers about the young boy who played the Garth Brooks songs. As my two brothers were both Garth Brooks fans, they were both excited when they discovered that a boy in school was playing his tunes on the guitar. As we arrived at our front door, my eldest brother was singing a Garth Brooks song. I bent down and recovered the front door key from under one of my mother's geranium pots. I opened the door and my two brothers followed me into the house. There appeared to be no one at home. My younger brother told me that he would love to be able to play the guitar and sing Garth Brooks songs. I told my brother to put the kettle on while I was dropping my school bag in my bedroom. When I reached my bedroom door and tried to open it, I realised that it was locked. I turned to my brothers and asked them if they had locked my bedroom door. They both shook their heads. I dropped my bag against the bedroom door and returned to the kitchen with my brothers. My brothers and I continued to discuss the young boy in school. Suddenly, my bedroom door opened and my father emerged. We turned around and looked at him in surprise. Our father had been eavesdropping on our conversation. It felt very strange. He turned on my younger brother immediately and struck him across the face with the back of his hand. Blood appeared from my younger brother's nose. My younger brother ran to the bathroom, crying. He told the other two of us that that would stop my younger brother yapping for a while. He asked us who we were talking about. We told him that we were discussing a young boy from the neighbourhood who played the guitar in school. My father said that no true musician copied another musician's work and to be deemed a real musician you had to compose your own songs. My father then told us that no one in the young boy's family had ever been able to play any musical instrument. He said that the boy would never succeed as there was no history of music in his family. My brother and I looked at our father and wondered why our father had developed such spite for a young boy he barely knew. We wondered if he was jealous of the young boy, but were afraid to say anything. Everything went quiet all of a sudden. My father sat down. Tony and I listened to Niall cleaning the blood off his nose in the bathroom. I went to my bedroom and threw my schoolbag in there. I noticed all my teddies were on the floor. It was like there had been a robbery in the room. My earrings were on the floor and my nightclothes were all over the place. I had a tiger bear in my bedroom. I noticed that someone had cut his tail and whiskers off . Several minutes later, my mother arrived home. When she heard Niall's sobs coming from the bathroom, she asked my father what had happened. My father merely ignored her and left the house. She then asked me what had happened. I told her that our father had struck Niall across the face because he was complimenting a young boy from the neighbourhood who could play the guitar. She entered the bathroom and tried to comfort Niall. What else could she do?

For the following few weeks, my father began going for long walks around the area. He had become concerned about his weight and was doing everything possible (other than giving up the drink) to lessen it. On several occasions, he asked me to accompany him on these long walks. He would generally bring me to the most remote areas in the locality and rape me. On every occasion, he threatened to hurt and even drown me if I told anybody what he was doing. Incidents of abuse at this time were not restricted to the outdoors. One afternoon, while I was ironing clothes for my mother, my father returned from the pub and told me to follow him into my bedroom. My two brothers were in the sitting room watching TV, oblivious to what was going on. I followed my father into my bedroom and he raped me on my bed. When he was finished, he began telling me simplistic stories trying to comfort me. When he looked at my face and realised my complexion was very pale he told me to go for a cycle on my bike and to return in an hour's time. When I returned home an hour later, my mother asked me where I had been. I told her I had been playing with one of my neighbours.

STRANGE NOISES IN THE NIGHT

Over the following week, as I slept, I began to hear strange noises in the night. When I told my parents about these noises at breakfast, they told me that I was imagining these sounds. For the following couple of nights, I decided to remain awake during the night and investigate what was causing these noises. On the first night, I heard the squeaks of a little animal at my bedroom door. As I lay in bed, I could hear the little animal's footsteps on the linoleum outside my bedroom. After ten minutes, the noises ceased. The following night, as I lay in bed, the little critter returned. Again, I could hear his little feet scratching on the linoleum. However, on this occasion, I decided to see if I could catch the little devil. I got out of bed and walked towards my bedroom door. I could still hear the little creature's footsteps outside the door. I opened the door as quickly as I could and spotted a little mouse looking in my direction. As soon as he realised the door had opened, he scampered off . I tried to follow him but he disappeared from view.

The following morning, I told my mother and father that I had spotted a mouse in the house the previous night. My mother said that she had also found some mouse droppings on the linoleum. She told my father to place a couple of traps down to catch the little devils. Several days later, my father caught a little mouse in one of the traps and that was the last time my furry little friends visited me during the night.

As my father was not working at this time (come to think of it, I don't think he ever worked), he spent much of the day in bed sleeping. My mother tried to motivate him but gradually began to accept the inevitable that she had married a man who was not fond of the word "work". During the day while he slept, he warned all of us to be as silent as we could be and not to disturb him from his sleep. At breakfast time, we were not allowed to eat until our father had arrived at the breakfast table.

On occasion, my two younger sisters sneaked into the kitchen and stole some Lega biscuits before my father arrived for breakfast. My mother knew what my two sisters were doing but decided to ignore their behaviour for the sake of some peace and quiet. At dinnertime, my father had got into the habit of commenting on the amount of food my mother placed on Niall's plate. My father constantly complained to my mother that she was overfeeding Niall and that he was a lazy so-and-so who didn't deserve to be receiving a meal intended for a grown man, let alone an adolescent boy. My mother asked my father why he constantly picked on Niall. My father merely ignored her and continued complaining.

In school, Niall was constantly getting into trouble. He thoroughly enjoyed being the centre of attention and went to any length to incur the headmaster's wrath. He was constantly setting traps and making fun of the teachers. On one occasion, he entered a classroom, grabbed the chalk, started writing on the blackboard and pretended to be a teacher. He told the class that their usual teacher was unwell and that he would be conducting lessons that day. He told the students to take out their books and read a certain page. A minute later, the real teacher entered the classroom. Niall merely smiled at the students and exited the classroom as quickly and as quietly as he could. On another occasion while I was playing basketball, a teacher approached me and asked me why my younger brother was constantly misbehaving in class and never had his homework done. I told the teacher that Niall was a joker and loved to make people smile. Shortly afterwards, Niall started working part-time in Maamcross.

He was turning turf at the weekends and gradually began to lose interest in school. After a while, Niall asked me if I would like to help him turning turf at the weekends. I was delighted as this provided me with the opportunity to be away from the family home at the weekends. I enjoyed my time with Niall on the bog as there was no one there telling us what to do all the time. When we were finished on the bog, I found it difficult to return home. At the time, I had decided that as soon as I got a job and could support myself that I would run away from my father and my home.

One night, as I lay in bed, I began to have difficulties with my breathing. I was having ongoing problems with my health and was quite frail at the time. When my mother heard me coughing in the bedroom, she rushed in. She noticed that my colour was off and that my complexion was very pale. She called my father and told him to bring me to Galway Hospital immediately. He told her not to worry that he would bring me as soon as he had a shower. When he was finished showering, he asked his uncle who was visiting at the time to help him carry me out to the car. While driving to Galway, my father and mother were stopped by the Police for speeding. When the police officer asked my father why he was speeding, my mother pointed to me in the back of the car. She said that she was bringing me to Galway Hospital as I was quite ill. The Police officer looked at me in the back of the car and realised that my mother was telling the truth. He asked my father if he wanted to call for an ambulance. My father said there was no need and that he would reach the hospital in ten minutes.

When we arrived at the hospital, I was immediately examined by a Doctor. The Doctor told my father that he needed to conduct blood tests to determine what was wrong with me. My father told my mother that he was dropping out for a quick pint and that he'd return within an hour. My mother sat at my bedside and awaited the test results. When my father returned two hours later, he asked my mother if the Doctor had returned with the blood tests. When my mother told him that the Doctor hadn't returned yet, my father proceeded down the hallway towards the Doctors office, entered, and asked the Doctor why the test results were taking so long. My mother and I could hear my father shouting. When my father returned to my bedside, he told me that the Doctor would be returning with my results within a matter of minutes. I was discharged from the hospital at 4am with some medication.

A week later as I lay on my bed playing with my favourite teddy Vefeen, my brother Tony entered my bedroom. He told me that he had read a story about a girl who couldn't sleep at night without a Teddy Bear. He said that playing with a teddy at my age was a sign of insecurity or that something had happened to me. He asked me "did I have the bears for support?" I told him that I did. A week later, I spotted some of my bears hanging on the trees at the back of our house. I had a nightdress on one of them and it was soaking wet. When I lifted the bear off the tree, I discovered that there was a very deep hole in its neck. I knew immediately that it was my father who had damaged my bear. When I came into the kitchen, I showed my mother the poor teddy. I told my mother that it was a good thing the teddies weren't alive to feel the pain of my father tearing their tails and putting holes in their necks or hanging them on the trees. There were other times he would take the bears and I would never find them. He would say to me 'not until you take that face off'.

One afternoon, I returned home from school and discovered that my favourite mascara had disappeared from my bedroom. Initially, I thought my mother had borrowed it. When I asked her, she told me that she hadn't taken it. Later that evening, the mystery was solved. When my father returned home, I spotted that the top of his head looked a little darker than usual. On closer inspection, I discovered that my father had drawn dark lines on his head to cover up his impending baldness. Although I was annoyed at losing my mascara, the comical sight of my father's head nearly made up for it. When I asked my father about my mascara, he told me that he would give me some money to buy two more. One for himself and one for me. He told me that he had lost faith in all the other hair growing remedies and was experimenting with the mascara.

One evening, Niall returned from the pub where he was working. Niall entered the sitting room where my siblings, mother and I were watching TV and told us that our father had dropped into the pub where he worked. He also told us that our father had given a bunch of young girls a lift from one pub to another. The following morning at breakfast, my mother asked my father who he had given a lift to the previous night. My father lied and said no one. My mother asked my father why Niall had told her that he had given a bunch of girls a lift to a pub the previous night. My father told my mother that Niall was mistaken. Later that evening, when Niall returned from work, my mother brought up the subject again. When my mother questioned Niall about the matter, my father winked at Niall. Niall looked confused and again told my mother that our father had given some girls a lift. Anger crossed my father's face. My mother asked what went on and who were the girls that were in the car. My father changed his original story and told her he had given a ride to a few girls that worked with Niall. My father gave Niall a threatening look.

Shortly afterwards, my father brought me to a pub in Galway city. This was gradually to become a common occurrence. Before we left the house, my father told me to tell my mother that I wanted to accompany him to the pub. He warned me on a few occasions if I didn't go with him that I would pay for it the next day. On our way to the pub in the car he told me that he would never do this to me again and how sorry he was. On our way home from the pub, he pulled up a lane near Forbaigh and raped me in the car. The evil had made me believe with his crocodile tears that he would never do this again. He used to tell me strange stories in the car about when he was a child. He mentioned to me that he had an aunt that touched his private part. I didn't know whether to believe him or not but it still didn't give him the right to abuse me.

He told me there was no point for me to be looking forward to my 18th Birthday as I would still be under his control. He told me that I might not be alive then if I didn't keep my mouth shut. He told me that he could put me in a place where nobody would ever find me. He said that he was capable of doing this without leaving a trace behind. At this stage, I was afraid of my father

I remember another night when we were driving from Clifden. On our way home, my father pulled in at the side of a road. I got an awful feeling that I would never make it home. He turned the car lights off and parked outside an unlit house. He pointed to a child's bicycle and told me that my younger sister Grainne's birthday was the following day and that he had to get that bike. He jumped out of the car, walked over to the front gate, lifted the bike and came back to the car. He opened the boot and threw the small bike in it. He jumped back into the car, keeping his eye on both mirrors as we drove off to ensure that we wouldn't be followed.

As soon as he got out of bed the next morning, he told my younger sister Grainne that he had got her a lovely birthday present. She jumped with joy and asked him what it was. He said "let me put it like this to you, its something that you have always wanted. I bought it in Galway yesterday. Before I give it to you, you have to promise to take care of it. You won't get it for three hours because I have to do some work on it." He then called Niall and told him to get a knife. My father and Niall then went into the shed. After an hour, my father emerged and called my sister Grainne into the shed. My sister jumped with joy as soon as she saw her new bike. She jumped on her bike and flew down the hill.

One afternoon, I asked my mother if she would buy me a keyboard as I needed one to practice on. My mother said that she would buy it in a shop called The Four Corners in Galway city. My father insisted on coming with us. On our journey to Galway city, my father beeped the horn on his car at several female drivers. He enjoyed insulting them and telling my mother that women shouldn't be allowed on the roads. When we arrived in Galway city, my father insisted on accompanying us into the music store. As soon as we entered, my father spotted an accordion and brought us over to look at it. My father asked the shop assistant how much it cost. He nearly keeled over when she told him the price. My mother looked at my father and told him that we were in Galway city to buy a keyboard. At the time, I knew my mother had little money so I made sure that I chose a relatively inexpensive keyboard. My mother did her shopping in the city centre before we left. On our way home, my father stopped at a pub in Galway for a few drinks. When mam complained, he asked us to join him. At the time, I was only interested in going home and practicing on my new keyboard.

Shortly afterwards, my father brought Tony and I to a funfair in Carraroe village. My father spent the whole day in the pub. When the funfair finished, Tony and I decided to try and locate our father. We dropped into the pub and spotted our father beside a man that was playing an accordion. My father asked him if could he play both rows on the accordion? My father borrowed the accordion from him and began to play, trying to find a tune he liked. Tony told me my father would be happy as soon as he got the chance to express himself in public. People were surprised that he played so well. The man who owned the accordion asked my father the name of the tune he was playing and the name of the artist. My father told him that he preferred to compose his own tunes, not copy other artists work. He was happy going home.

Saving On The Electricity Bill

We never received a high Electricity bill at home. My father had managed to devise a scheme whereby the electric meter outside our home never seemed to rise. This of course created suspicion when the man from the ESB read our meter. On one particular occasion, one of our neighbours spotted my father fiddling with the meter. My father merely smiled at the woman and continued what he was doing. When he entered the house, he told my mother that the woman wouldn't know what the cable was for. Anytime I wanted to have a shower, he told me not to go near the bath until he put the lead up to stop the meter from working. He also told my mother not to be cooking and using electricity until he had the lead fixed to the meter box. He used to join the cable from the white box on the inside of the door out through the hole on the back door to the white box where the meter used to be checked. I recall one day, a man from the ESB walked up to our gate. He was around to check the meter. My father jumped off the chair that was beside the window and dragged the grey cable out of the meter box on the wall. I could see sparks popping from it. He rushed out to the back and took it out of the white box. He was sweating nervously. He was lucky that he didn't get caught.

One Sunday afternoon, my father brought Tony out in the car for a driving lesson. At the time, my father was driving an automatic BMW. My brother was under the impression that he was a professional driver like our father. Tony told me that there was no way he would ever crash as my father was such a good teacher. While my father was giving Tony instructions, my sisters and I were in the back seat. As my brother turned right, he went straight into the drain. My father grabbed the steering wheel and tried to control the car. However my brother banged into a rock. My sisters screamed in the back. I smiled, knowing that my brother had managed to crash the car and cost my father a packet (less money for him to spend in Galway pubs). My father told Tony not to worry that he could fix the car. If my youngest brother had crashed the car he would have been on death row. My father said "we will give Barbara a go now to drive. I know she will be a mad driver like I was". My father was shocked when I sat behind the wheel of the automatic BMW and drove fast down Muicineach lane. He told my siblings that I drove like he did when he was my age. He was laughing about the way I drove. I wasn't a bit nervous. My brother told me if my father was doing 100mph in the car that he wouldn't be afraid sitting on the passenger seat. My mother was the same. She never feared sitting beside my father in the car when he was driving at speed. There were nights I lay awake wondering how my father managed to drive home in his car, considering the amount of pints he had taken. Many nights, I wished that my mother would get the news that my father had crashed his car. God forgive me for saying that, but at the time that's how I felt. Most of the people were afraid to take their cars out at Christmas because the roads were icy. But my father didn't care about road conditions.

As Christmas approached, we received our holidays from school. Several of the girls from my class constantly chatted about the local youth club and which boy they had kissed. I envied them, but said nothing. My father had given me permission to attend the local youth club on two occasions, chaperoned by Tony on each occasion. As the class dispersed for Christmas, one of my classmates asked me if I would be attending the youth club that night, as it was a special occasion to mark the Christmas holidays. I told her that I would have to ask my parents. When I returned home from school, I asked my mother if I could attend the club later that night. She told me that I would have to ask my father. I knew what his answer would be. When my father arrived home later that evening, I asked him if I could go. When he said no, I started to cry. Both my parents merely ignored my pleadings. As I sat on the settee watching TV later that night, my father entered the room and told me to tell my mother that I wanted to drop down to the pub with him. As I spoke to my mother in the kitchen, I could hear my father at the door listening to every word I said. As we drove off in the car, my father started to discuss his past, as usual. He complained about having married my mother and how he wished he could live his life over. We stopped at a pub in Carna and my father tried to make me drink a glass of whiskey. I hated the smell of it and nearly vomited when I sipped it. I told him that I was too young to be drinking and that I wanted to have a glass of orange. As there were people in the pub, he didn't make a scene (he was too clever for that). After he had a couple of drinks in Carna, he looked at me and told me that we were heading off to another pub. This time, he drove many miles away from where we lived to a pub where nobody recognised him. Again he tried to make me drink whiskey, again I refused. As he drank, his mood, gradually changed. First he was apologising about his behaviour towards me, then he was cursing my mother's family. It was like a seesaw, one side then the other. When we were finished in the second pub, my father drove towards our home. On the way, my father told me that he had been sexually abused as a child. At this stage, I never believed anything he told me. He started to cry and apologised for hurting me. He swore that he would never do it again. He then asked me if I could remember when he started interfering with me. I told him I couldn't remember. He then said that he had only started a few months ago. Although my mind was addled at this stage of my life, I knew the abuse had started years earlier. I had no idea why he was saying this to me. Hoping that he wouldn't hurt me, I merely nodded in agreement and hoped that he would drive directly home and leave me alone. He then looked at me and said, "I guess you will turn around sooner or later and tell people what I did to you. I know you will always have a mark in your mind, but remember I can always put you in a place where nobody will ever find your body......so keep your mouth shut...." Before we arrived at the house, my father turned the car off a by-road and raped me. When he was finished, he slumped over and fell asleep. I sat in the car for the next three hours waiting for him to wake and bring me home.

I spent most of the following day in my bedroom, practicing on my keyboard. I had received musical notes for several songs when my mother had bought the keyboard for me. I was gradually learning how to play some of the tunes. As I played, I sang. After a while, my father began shouting at me, telling me that I'd never make a living out of my singing. As ever, there was absolutely no encouragement for anything. When my father continued complaining about the noise I was making, my mother entered my bedroom and told me to wait until my father had gone out before I started playing again. She told me that I should forget about music for the moment and that if I still felt the same way when I was older that I should take it up again.

When visitors came into the house, my father watched me like a hawk. If he wasn't sitting in their company, he would sit in his bedroom next door and listen to what was being said. I began to practice on an accordion Tony had borrowed from our uncle next door. Tony was doing well on the accordion. He had notes and used to practice tunes. I used to learn from him at home. An elderly man from the neighbourhood visited on occasion and thoroughly enjoyed our playing. When my brother asked my father to help him with the accordion, my father told him that he couldn't read notes and could only play by ear. After a while, my younger sister also began playing the accordion. Nearly everyone in our house knew how to play it.

Gradually my health and to some degree my sanity began to give way. I was beginning to spend as much time in hospital as I spent at home. One night, I had severe stomach pain. I sat in the bed hoping that it would pass. It didn't. I decided I no longer wanted to suffer. I grabbed a bottle of pills that were on my dressing table that had been prescribed for my kidney problem. I opened the bottle and swallowed the entire contents with the help of a glass of water. As I lay in bed, I began to shiver. The pain eased and I felt a numbing sensation. I felt I had no reason to live and perhaps every reason not to. Whenever I showed an interest in anything, I was constantly mocked and suppressed. At the time, the answer was quite obvious. However, fate was to intervene. Suddenly, I began to vomit uncontrollably. The entire contents of my stomach spewed forth. My two brothers, who had been watching TV in the sitting room, heard me vomiting and rushed into my bedroom. When they realised what was happening, they panicked a little, ran out, and returned carrying a bucket for me to get sick in. My eldest brother was practically crying and obviously concerned. They were only children, like myself, and had no idea how to respond to such a situation. The pills hadn't done the job. I wasn't sure whether I was relieved or not. At least the throbbing pain in my stomach had eased. When my parents returned home later that night, my two brothers told them that I had spent the entire night vomiting. When my parents entered my bedroom, they were taken aback by my sickly pallor. The following day, my mother brought me to the doctor. The doctor asked me what had happened. I didn't mention taking the tablets. I told him that I didn't feel well. The doctor spoke to my parents and told them that he was going to have me admitted to University College Hospital Galway for tests and observation. In a sense, this incident proved to be a very significant moment in my life as my father had obviously realised that neither my body or mind could tolerate any further abuse. I spent the following two weeks in hospital. When I returned home, I was very weak.

My father made no attempt to abuse me. A week later, my mother allowed me to return to school. In March, I started to study for my mock Junior Cert exam. Weeks passed and my father made no effort to approach me. At this time, I had been prescribed various types of medication for my symptoms. Sadly, none of the medical experts who examined me realised what was the cause of my illness. A pity.

Weeks later, as I sat watching TV, my father commented on my complexion. He told me that the medication the doctor had recently prescribed for my stomach was doing wonders for my looks. As ever, I was stunned by my father's insensitivity. He went into my bedroom and returned with several packets of pills. At the time, I had been prescribed various medication for my condition. He asked me to show him the one the doctor had most recently prescribed. I pointed to the tablets. When I told my mother about the conversation I had with my father that evening, she told me to ignore my father's comments and that I was a naturally pretty young girl. The following morning, my father went to the doctor's surgery. He told the doctor that he was suffering from the same symptoms as I was and he asked the doctor to prescribe the same medication. Bizarrely, the doctor believed him and prescribed the same tablets (truth is sometimes stranger than fiction). When my father returned home and told me what he did, I was speechless. My father's complexion didn't improve over the next few weeks. At this time, my mother convinced my father to sell our house in Kinvarra. She told him that she wanted to move away from his family who lived next door to us. My siblings and I were very surprised when we spotted the FOR SALE sign outside our house on our way to school one morning. When I arrived in school that morning, I told my friends that my parents were selling our house. Later that afternoon, during a break in classes, I began to vomit. When my English teacher entered the classroom, she realised I was in difficulty and brought me to the bathroom where I vomited. She then brought me to the Teachers Room and asked me to take a seat beside the window. She told me that she was going to ring one of my neighbour's and ask them to drop in and tell my parents what had happened. At that time, we still hadn't a phone in our home. As I sat in the Teachers room, my English teacher asked me if this was the first time that this had happened. I told her that I was having problems with my tummy. She sat and chatted with me until my parents arrived in the car. My father then drove me to the local doctor. The doctor prescribed further medication, then told my parents that my symptoms were more to do with the mind than the body and suggested to my parents that I should attend a child psychiatrist in Galway city. The doctor said that he could arrange it if my parents agreed. A look of concern crossed my father's face the instant the doctor suggested the possibility of a psychiatrist.

THE CHILD
PSYCHIATRIST

Three weeks later, we received a letter in the post from the doctor with details of my appointment with the child psychiatrist. I was supposed to attend the following week. At the time, we had students staying in our house and my mother told my father that he would have to bring me to Galway city for my appointment. The day before my appointment, my father spoke to me in the kitchen. He told me to tell the psychiatrist that I was being bullied in school and that was contributing to my stress and stomach symptoms. To tell the truth, my jacket had been ripped in school, but like all other school goers this was normal fare and had little impact on me. The following morning, my father and I headed off for Galway city. On the journey, my father told me again to tell the psychiatrist that I was being bullied and under no circumstances to mention that he had interfered with me if I knew what was good for me.

When we arrived in Galway, my father sat in the car while I attended my appointment with the Child Psychiatrist. When I entered the Psychiatrist's office, she asked me to take a seat.

She asked me several questions about myself. She asked me about my school, my family, my eating habits, my hobbies, my friends and various other issues. When she asked me about myself, I told her that I hated my image. She then asked me why I hated my image. I was unable to respond. When we were finished, she told me that she was arranging another appointment for the following week. I thanked her as I left. When I returned to the car, my father appeared very anxious.

On our way home, he asked me what I had said to the psychiatrist. I told him that the conversation was private and that the psychiatrist had told me not to speak to anybody about our conversation. I also told him that the psychiatrist had arranged another appointment for me for the following week. My father's demeanour and approach had changed. He no longer threatened me. He merely probed and continued to question me about the conversation I had had with the psychiatrist.. When he realised that I had no intention of discussing the matter with him, he changed the subject and told me that he would drop me in the following week.

A week later, I had my second appointment. On this occasion, my father accompanied me into the psychiatrist's office and sat in on my counselling session. As soon as the session began, my father started to interrupt and answer questions for me. He totally dominated the session and I sat there silently as he answered for me. He told the psychiatrist that I was being bullied in school. When the psychiatrist told him that I had said that I was happy in school, he became angry and started to rant. He told her that my expensive leather jacket had been slashed with a knife and that 3 separate schoolbags had been ripped and that two boys in my class were constantly calling me names like dogface. He then told the psychiatrist that he had complained to the school principal on three separate occasion regarding other students behaviour towards me. When she asked him if everything was OK at home and how I got on with my mother and siblings, he looked in my direction and told her that everything was fine. She then asked him if I was having any difficulties with my diet as she had read a report from Galway Hospital that indicated that I was having such difficulties. My father looked at me again and said that I was no longer having any such problems and that my eating habits were fine. When the session was over, she asked my father if I would be able to attend the following week. My father said that he was concerned that some of my classmates would discover that I was attending counselling and would think that I was insane. When the psychiatrist told my father that all counselling sessions were treated with the utmost confidentiality, my father said that he was afraid that if my classmates discovered that I was attending counselling, that they would mock me even more and that life could become unbearable for me. I sat and listened as he lied. Although my father had few other talents, he was without doubt the greatest and most plausible liar I had ever came across in my entire life.

He then said that he felt it would be better for me to end the sessions and thanked the psychiatrist for all her help. As soon as we returned to the car, my father smiled at me and said, "That's how you handle smart people." We drove back home. My counselling sessions had ended before they had began.

My First Job

Several weeks later, my brother managed to get me a job in the evenings where he was working. Most evenings the manager where I was working collected my brother and I and brought us to the job. The work was enjoyable and for the first time in my life, I had some money to spend. One evening, on our way to the job, my brother asked the manager if he had a job for my father. The manager told my brother to tell my father to drop in the following evening and the manager would see what he could do. The following evening, our father drove us to the job. The manager told my father that he could start immediately. The manger directed my father to the back of the building and showed him what he was supposed to do. After a couple of weeks, my father began complaining to the boss about the money he was earning. He sent my younger brother to the boss complaining about the wages. He thought he was entitled to the same amount of money as I was earning. There was a bonus system in operation in the factory and anyone who reached a certain target would receive it. My father became angry when he discovered that I had been well paid on two consecutive weeks. My father sent my younger brother to the boss to complain again about the amount of money he was earning. The boss asked my brother why my father couldn't complain himself. When my father finally mustered enough courage to approach the boss, he told the boss that the £75.00 that he was paid wouldn't feed an alien on a wet day. The boss suggested that my father should leave if he wasn't happy with the pay and conditions which my father duly did. On this occasion, my father had managed to hold down a job for three entire weeks, practically a record.

Although, I was working and earning a decent wage for the first time, I wasn't eating well at home and my general health was suffering. Shortly after my father was released from his contract of employment, I was rehospitalised. I was admitted to the Obstetrics and Gynaecological Department of University Hospital Galway where several tests were conducted on me. It was quite an interesting experience for a fifteen year old girl. The nurses began to think that I was a diabetic when they noticed that I had lots of sweets and fizzy drinks in my cupboard. They were surprised when they saw the amount of visitors that visited me. The Doctors told me that my test results indicated that there was nothing medically wrong with me. I was annoyed because I knew I had an underlying medical problem. One afternoon, as I was walking along the hospital corridor, the matron told me that I walked like an old lady. She was right. I was like an old person. I ached all over. While I was in hospital, my father visited me while he was frequenting Galway city pubs at night. When he visited me, he told me to walk along the hospital corridors with him in order to create the impression that we had a loving relationship. He became angry when I refused. After spending three weeks in hospital, I returned home. My mother noticed that my health wasn't improving. She panicked and told the Doctor that something had to be done as I was only drinking tea in the morning with a piece of toast. The Doctor told her that the results were coming out clear and that he had liaised with several specialists in Galway to find out what was wrong with me. He said that they all told him that I was as clear as a doll inside. However, they suggested that stress or anxiety may be contributing to my unexplained medical condition. My father was anxious and decided to seek advice from his neighbours. One neighbour told him "When you have toothache you know the problem is in your mouth. The same thing with Barbara's tummy, no doubt". Tony told me that there was nothing wrong with me other than stress. I told him that I would prove to him that there was something medically wrong with me that the doctors were not aware of yet. My mother took me to a specialist in Galway and begged him to do something. She told him that she was fed up running in and out of the casualty dept of UCHG watching me sitting on a trolley all night. The doctor told her that he would send me back to Galway Hospital and carry out a scope test. Days later, I was admitted to the Hospital and the same examinations were carried out on me. On this occasion, they discovered that there was acid leaking from my tummy. They didn't know where the acid was coming from. They told my mother that they didn't have the appropriate facilities to carry out the relevant tests on me and were going to send me to Beaumont Hospital in Dublin to carry out further tests to establish where the unexplained acid was emanating from.

After two weeks, I received a letter asking me to attend an examination in Dublin. When I asked my mother if she would bring me, she told me she had to look after the students and that my father would have to bring me. When the ordained morning arrived, we took the morning train from Galway to Dublin. On the train journey to Dublin, I burst out crying because my father was constantly warning me not to say anything to the doctors in Dublin. When several other passengers became concerned and asked why I was crying, my father became worried and told them that I was frightened as I was going to Dublin for medical tests. Shortly afterwards, my father headed to the bar area. He returned after half an hour and gave me a bottle of orange and a bar of chocolate. As the train approached Dublin, his mood changed and he tried to comfort me, telling me everything would be fine. When we arrived at Heuston Station, we took a taxi from the station to Beaumont hospital in the centre of Dublin. When we arrived at Beaumont hospital, a Doctor greeted us. After a while, the doctor brought me into a room and conducted several tests on me. Before I left, the Doctor placed two thin wires through my nostrils. It felt very uncomfortable, but the Doctor said that I would have to leave the wires in my nose until the following day. He also placed a 24hr monitor on my body and told me that he would remove it the following day also. When I was finished, the Doctor told my father that I would have to return the following day and have the wires removed. He also told my father that he would have the result of my tests the following day. The Doctor then told my father that he would arrange a Bed and Breakfast for us that was very close to the hospital. While the Doctor was on the phone to the proprietor of the B&B, the Doctor asked me if I would like to share the same bedroom with my father for the night. I told him that I would prefer to have my own separate room. The Doctor booked two separate rooms for us. As we were leaving the clinic, my father's mood changed. He became angry and asked me in a threatening manner why I had asked for a separate room. I told him that I wanted to sleep in a room on my own.

That afternoon, I went around Dublin city shopping. My father took me into a bar that evening. I told him that I wasn't well and that I wanted to go back to the B&B. He took me back to the bed and breakfast. The Doctor had asked me to fast from midnight. The following morning, as the Doctor removed the cables from my nose, my father sat outside the door. The surgeon asked me questions about how I had been getting on. The next thing he noticed the test result coming out. He was surprised and told me that there was a large build up of acid in my stomach that was escaping and inflaming my chest walls. He told me that it was inexcusable that I hadn't been treated for this condition for such a long time and that he was sending a report to the relevant people in Galway Hospital to ensure that my condition would be dealt with immediately. He also told me that I looked sad and he asked me if there was something else bothering me. I told him there was. I couldn't really talk and I lowered my voice. I pointed in the direction of the door as I was sure my father was listening. The Doctor rose quickly and rushed to open the door. He spotted my father rushing back to his seat outside the room. I was very frightened in case my father had overheard something. The Doctor was surprised and told my father that I would be out in a couple of minutes. He asked me again if I wished to speak to him about anything that might be bothering me. I felt comfortable with the elderly man. He seemed to be a nice Doctor. I opened up to him. I told him that there was something hurting me. He watched my reaction as I spoke. He told me that it must be bad if I had such difficulty speaking about it. I told him that it was bad. He wrote something on the report and told me that I would be seeing some nice Doctors in Galway shortly. I thanked him for his help and left.

An hour later, my father and I returned to Heuston Station where we boarded the train for Galway. When we returned home, my father told my mother about the results. The next day, my neighbour came in and told us there was a call requesting me to attend Galway Hospital the following day. My neighbour said that they must have found something wrong as they had called me so quickly. The following morning, my parents drove me to the hospital. The Doctor told my mother to take a seat with me in the room while he was waiting for the specialist to arrive. The nurses stood beside the specialist when he stepped into the room. He pulled the curtains and looked at me sitting up on the bed. He turned and said to the nurse

"Is this the girl who's having trouble at home". My mother immediately jumped off the chair and

approached the doctor and asked him "What do you mean by my daughter having some trouble at home." He looked at her and apologised and said that he had mixed me up with another patient. I knew the doctor who had examined me in Beaumont had forwarded comments of my visit to Dublin to the Doctors in Galway. The surgeon told her that he was certain that my symptoms were stress related due to the level of acid in my stomach. My mother remonstrated with the doctor insisting that there was something medically wrong me and that it was not psychological.

I was kept in hospital for three weeks. They operated on a valve in my tummy that was leaking acid into my chest. I couldn't walk for days after the operation. I felt very weak and sore all over and had difficulties eating. The doctors were surprised and couldn't understand why I wasn't eating after my surgical procedure. A dietician visited me and asked me why I wasn't eating. I merely lay in the bed, listlessly. After my operation, I was transferred from the maternity ward to another ward.

A couple of weeks after I was released from hospital, I was re-admitted complaining of severe headaches. My Granny, and aunty and uncle on my mother's side visited me. My granny left the hospital room, I was staying in, in floods of tears when she realised how thin I had become. Several days later she returned and asked my mother if she could bring me to a spiritual healer, who she believed had a special gift with sick people. My granny told my mother that she suspected that one of my ribs had collapsed due to the length of time I hadn't been eating. She told the nurses that she needed to bring me out for a couple of hours. When we arrived at the old cottage where the old man lived, I intuitively sensed that he had a gift. He told my mother that a part of my rib had collapsed. He told my mother that was the reason I was constantly short of breath. He placed his hands between my ribs and slowly worked down to the one that was affected. I felt him doing something that relieved the pain. I felt better when I left his home. My mother offered him money. He told her not to insult the gift of healing by offering money. He told her that he would accept some tobacco. She rushed out and bought him that. He was very nice to me. My granny drove my mother and I back to the hospital. I was very grateful for my granny's intervention.

I felt like I had been in hospital for a long time when I eventually returned home. I was very thin. My mother asked me if I wanted to sit my Junior Cert examinations or defer them until the following year as I had missed much of the academic school year. I decided to return to school and complete the last two months of third year. When the examinations finally arrived, I was very nervous. On the first morning of my examinations, I sat at the mirror in my bedroom and prayed and lit a candle on my dressing table and asked for God's help. I couldn't believe it when I received my results in September. I passed most of the exams. My friends were surprised when I showed them my results. I had achieved relatively good results even though I had missed the best part of the school year due to my ongoing medical issues. When I asked my parents if I could attend the local youth club with my classmates that evening to celebrate my Junior Cert, my father insisted that my elder brother chaperone me for the night. My father told me to be careful who I spoke to. When I arrived at the youth club, most of my classmates were already there. During the night, a boy asked me out onto the floor for a slow dance. I was practically shaking on the floor. The young boy sensed my anxiety and told me not to worry that it was only a dance. When the first song finished, I rushed off the dance floor. The young boy looked quite surprised by my behaviour. I spent the rest of the night chatting to my friends under my brother's ever watchful eye. The following morning at breakfast, my father asked me why I had been dancing with strangers. I told him that it was only one dance. He told me to be careful in future, especially of married men who were constantly looking to take advantage of young naïve girls. I merely nodded and finished my breakfast.

MOVING HOUSE

A couple of weeks later, my parents received a buyer for our house. I was happy to leave Kinvarra. Some friends of my parents offered us the use of a house in Muicineach, a small village not too far from Kinnvarra, until we bought another house. As soon as we moved into our new rented accommodation, one of our neighbours dropped in and welcomed my mother. The lady had two daughters who were around my age. When my father discovered that I was playing with her daughters, he told the woman that I was a liar and that she shouldn't believe a word out of my mouth. I was angry when I overheard him telling the woman that I was a liar. One evening as my mother chatted to our neighbour, my father entered the sitting room and told my mother that he was heading out for the evening. When my mother asked him if he would bring her out to the Country and Western night that was on in Carraroe, he told her that he had no interest in that type of music and that she would have to make her own way there if she wanted to go. My mother blushed. The neighbour stood up and told my mother that she had to leave. My mother, defeated as ever, merely accepted my father's behaviour and returned to watching the TV. My father headed out the door.

When I asked my mother if she was going to drop down to Carraroe for the music, she looked at me blankly and said that she no longer felt like going out.

The next Sunday, my mother and Tony went to Carraroe shopping. While she was in Carraroe, she was approached by her father who she hadn't seen for a couple of years. When my mother returned home that afternoon she was as happy as I had seen her in a long while. She told my father who was getting ready to go out again for the evening that her father was dropping around to bring her out for a few drinks to catch up on things. My father seemed annoyed that she had contacted her father. I was home alone with my brothers and sisters that evening. I was singing in the house and I had fun playing with my siblings.

The following morning, a row erupted at breakfast. My father wasn't happy that my mother had stayed out til the early hours with her father in the pub. My mother told her that she had no option as my father never brought her out. She also said that she had a great night with her father. My father, bitter as ever, reminded her of the occasion when my mother had met her father a couple of years earlier and her father showed no interest in her and that there was no evidence that he was her biological father. My mother told my father that she was delighted that she had met her father again and that nothing he could say would change that. However, my father continued tormenting my mother until she eventually left the kitchen in tears. I followed my mother into her bedroom and told her not to listen to her spiteful husband. When I returned to the kitchen, I overheard my father suggesting to Niall that my mother was having an affair with her own father. I knew my father was a sick individual, but this was even a new departure for him. Moments later, my mother returned to the kitchen and told my father that if he said one more bad word about her father that she would spend the rest of the day in the pub with her father. For the first time in my mother's life she was no longer alone and my father realised that he was going to lose this battle and would never be able to touch my mother again. Later that afternoon, my mother's father arrived outside our front gate. He did not enter our house but waited until my mother went out to him. Seconds later, the car pulled off. My father was accustomed to bullying women, not men who were several inches taller than him. As soon as my mother left, my father started insulting her father. He would of course never insult this man to his face.

Weeks went by and my father began to complain that there was no privacy in the house. He went on about the lady next door visiting us all the time. My mother spoke to him about the possibility of moving to Carraroe. My father told her that he didn't want to move nearer her father and that he knew that was her plan all the time. My father had no desire to relocate to Carraroe and pressurised my mother into asking her friend in Ballinahowen near Tully to lease one of his houses to us until my parents decided where to buy a house.

Weeks later, my father got his wish and we moved to Rosamhil, Ballinahowen near Tully. A few days after the move, my mother's father visited us. This was the first time that I had ever seen these two men under the same roof. When my grandfather entered the house, he handed my sisters and I a couple of boxes of chocolates. He then took a seat in the sitting room and started chatting with my mother and I. My father was in the kitchen speaking with Tony, making uncomplimentary comments about my grandfather. This trait seemed to be an idiosyncrasy that ran in my father's family, talking about people behind their backs. An adolescent as ever. Shortly afterwards, my mother and grandfather went off for a drive.

Around the same time, my brother and I were invited to attend a social night with our work colleagues. On the night of the function, my father told us he was going to come along. I wore a long black velvet dress. My younger brother and I spent most of the night jiving. We both weren't aware that there was a jiving competition. We won a prize for our jiving. Every time, I looked at the bar I noticed my father standing in the corner watching me like a hawk. He wanted to ensure that no man was talking to me. A young man I knew from the locality walked up to me and told me that my father had a nice job. I asked him what he meant? He said "Well, he appears to be watching you all the time." I was surprised that somebody had spotted him. He told me that he would have to leave my company very quickly as my father had been giving him dirty looks. At the end of the night my father asked me what the young man had said to me. I told him that he had inquired after my brother Tony.

The following weekend, I returned home late after spending the night in a local pub with one of my friends. It was 1am when I knocked on my front door. At first, no one answered the door. Eventually the door opened. My parents attacked me and started hitting me with the soles of their shoes. They kept hitting me over the head with the shoes. When Tony heard the commotion that was occurring in my parents' bedroom he entered the room and was astounded by the sight that was unfolding before his very eyes. He screamed at my parents to stop hitting me on the head with the shoes. My father kept hitting me and told my mother to slap me across the face. They pulled my hair and nearly suffocated me on their bed. The following morning, at breakfast I didn't speak. I sat in the room distant when my father walked in. He kept reminding me of the English girl I had been palling around with had a dysfunctional family history and that I shouldn't be associating with her. I liked her and didn't respond to him. He told my mother that my friend was using me to attract men.

Weeks later, my father gave out to me for going around in a car with my English pal. He told my mother that I wasn't obeying the house rules. He suggested that they would have to become more strict with me. He went out drinking that afternoon. He came home intoxicated at 10pm. That was unusual for my father to come home early from the pub. I presumed there was a thunder storm on the way. Tony sat in the kitchen chatting to him. I walked in the kitchen to put the kettle on and my father began to talk about the man from Carraroe who apparently fancied me. He opened his major cigarettes as he told me that he was drinking with the young man's uncle and that he assumed that he might be a nice man. He suddenly turned on me and said "that doesn't give you the right or the permission to go near him. Tony is here with me and he will keep a close eye on you in the pubs and he will tell who you associate with." He told me to stay away from the English girl. I didn't listen to him at all. He told my mother that the best they could come up with was to move away again. He told her that the owners of the house were visiting all the time and that he had no privacy. He said that he was sorry that he had ever sold the house in Kinnvarra as we didn't have any visitors and he could do whatever he wanted without any interference.

CARRAROE

My father told my mother that it was time we moved out of the area. Every time I thought I would settle down, my father wanted to move again. Eventually, my parents decided to leave Ballinahowen and lease a house in Carraroe. My mother told my father that Carraroe would be closer to shops and the local amenities. Although my father had misgivings about the move, it was apparent that my mother was delighted to be moving nearer to her father's house. As soon as we moved into the house, my father told me not to be spending time with some of my friends and not to engage with any of the young men from the village. As I sat there reading the paper, my father became very angry when he realised that I wasn't listening to him. At this stage, I had developed a sense of selective hearing when it came to my father's comments. He called my mother into the room and asked her to speak to me. She merely repeated my father's comments.

Shortly afterwards, my father made changes to the fireplace. Within a few weeks, our new home seemed quite cosy. After a couple of weeks, my mother managed to redecorate our new home. However, it wasn't long before my father sourced a problem. The electric meter. The meter required constant feeding (cash only) and my father was unaccustomed to paying for this service. Eventually, he decided enough was enough. He devised a scheme where he punctured a hole in a coin, ran a string through the coin and simply used the same coin all the time for topping up the electric meter. Weeks later, when the landlord visited, he opened the meter and was surprised at the scarcity of coins in the meter. When my father returned later that evening, my mother told my father that the landlord had been around checking the meter. She said she had been very embarrassed when the landlord opened the meter and only a few coins fell out. My father merely laughed and said "at least he knows that he won't be getting much money from us anyways, so he'll have to make profit elsewhere".

The following day, my sister Grainne and I went for a walk into town after dinner. As we approached a shop, my father's car stopped in front of us. My father asked us where we were going. We told him that we were going for a walk. My father then sped off in the car. As we continued walking, my sister turned towards me and asked me why my father had been asking her peculiar questions. When I asked her what she meant, she said that our father had recently started asking her questions about the conversations she had with me. She told me that she had told our father that we talked about nothing in particular, perhaps music more than anything else. At the time, I would have loved to explain to my sister what had happened to me. It would have been such a relief to tell someone and would have explained exactly why my father was asking such questions. However, I merely shook my head and kept on walking.

Shortly afterwards, a letter arrived for Tony in the house. As my mother lifted the letter off the ground, she said she thought it was from a university for Tony. My father took the letter from her, ripped it in two and threw it into the fire and said that Tony didn't need to go to any university. My mother stood there flabbergasted and told my father that Tony was awaiting that letter. I was disgusted with him for tearing Tony's letter which he had no business to open.

June, 1997

At the beginning of June, my mother was working part-time with her friend minding students. I had now left school and was working full-time and earning a decent wage and paying half the rent at home. One evening when I finished work, my father arrived outside my workplace and offered me a lift home. Although I would have preferred to share a minibus home with some of my work colleagues, I decided to accompany my father home in the car. As soon as I sat on the passenger seat, I could smell the alcohol wafting from my father's direction. He told me that he was around the Spiddal area and that he had waited to collect me. As we drove out of my workplace, he told me that he had to unwind and to have two pints in Spiddal after spending most of the day working on the bog. As he spoke to me, he drove down Rosamhil road and took the opposite turn from home and drove me towards the beach. I asked him why he wasn't driving straight home as my mother probably had the dinner on. He told me that he wanted to talk to me. He stopped the car on the beach. I panicked when he reminded me of the sexual abuse. I asked him what he wanted to know regarding it. He told me that he needed to know if I remembered every time he abused me.

He alleged that the abuse occurred on very few occasions. To appease him, I told him that I had no recollection whatsoever of the abuse. I knew that's what he wanted to hear. He kept pestering me in the car and said "well, I bet you after all my efforts not doing this to you for the past couple years that its still on your mind." I told him that I didn't remember and that I didn't want to talk about it. He told me to promise him that I wouldn't tell anybody. He told me to take my clothes off and to put the seat back. I told him that I thought he had stopped completely with the abuse. He told me that it wouldn't make any difference to me that I still looked moody and depressed. He asked me what was the point in stopping when I was manifesting all the signs that something had been done to me. He insisted that I take off my clothes. When I refused, he eventually relented. When he arrived home at 6.00pm, he told my mother that we had been delayed by an old friend. When he looked in my direction, I merely nodded.

The following morning, I went to work as usual. People noticed that I wasn't my usual talkative self and that I seemed to be distant and removed. When I finished work, one of my workmates told me that my father was outside again. I felt the shivers running down my spine. I was frightened, but knew that if I didn't go in the car with him that there would be trouble. When I sat in the car, I again smelled alcohol from my father's breath. He claimed that he was on his way out from Galway city after taking driving lessons on a truck. I knew this was merely an excuse for his presence. When he took a turn away from my home, I asked him where we were going. He said that he wanted to have a drink in Spiddal and that we would be heading home after that. When he parked outside a bar in Spiddal, he told me that he didn't want to park near the main road in case my brother Tony spotted the car on his way out of Galway on the bus. I told him that I was hungry and wanted to go home. He told me that I could have take-away food while he was in the pub. After a while, I got bored in the car after eating fries and listening to my favourite tapes. I went into the pub and my father told me to be patient and to wait until he'd finish his drink. He then bought me a glass of mineral water. After drinking his pint he told me that he was going to drive to Forbagh. I refused to go with him. I told him that I wanted to go home. He ignored my comments and brought me to another pub in Spiddal. After we left the second pub, he drove past my workplace in Inverin. He then drove the car down a lane. He pushed his seat back and pretended that he was tired. He kept saying that he knew that he hadn't been a good father to me but claimed that he wouldn't want to see my body wasted on another man. I became bored listening to him. I couldn't stop yawning in the car. He repeated the same story of the previous night about what I had remembered about the past. He said that he intended to leave me alone in the future. He pulled the car out and said that he would have his last pint in Inverin. I spent half an hour in the car waiting for him. I got tired of listening to music and eventually I went into the bar. He got a mineral drink for me and afterwards he kept insisting I order an alcoholic drink from the barman. I had to take a glass in the end. I was so ashamed of his behaviour in front of the barman. We left the pub before midnight. My father drove down towards Rosamhil Road, the same beach that we went to the previous evening. He kept telling me to undress and I told him to leave me alone. He told me that he would leave me alone and I was relieved when he drove back onto the main road. After a few minutes driving, he took a right turn down a laneway that was facing a lake. He stopped the car in the middle of the boithrin and asked me if I was going to keep refusing him. I told him to stop and bring me home. He then told me that I had always talked about committing suicide and that I should get out of the car and drown myself in the lake. I told him that I wouldn't do it without saying goodbye to my mother. I told him that I wouldn't drown myself in such an isolated area. He immediately locked the doors. I knew I had nowhere to go in the middle of nowhere. He told me to undress myself and when I refused he became very aggressive and put his two arms around my neck and began choking me.

He then took his hands off my neck and raped me. When he was finished, I thought that was the end of it. However, he then replaced his hands around my neck and started choking me again. When I looked at him, it appeared as if he was possessed. I felt my neck tightening and floods of tears coming from my eyes and my face boiling with heat as I felt him choking me. I was totally switched off from what was being done to me. I promised myself as I looked at the sky that if I survived that night that I would press charges. Suddenly, a light appeared outside the car and someone began knocking on the car door. My father panicked and moved back over to the driver's seat. I immediately opened the passenger door and vomited. A young man stood at the door and asked my father and I if we had a cigarette lighter. My neck felt sore and tight. My father searched for the ignition with his car keys and hurriedly told the man that he had no lighter. The young man stood there looking directly at my father's face. My father's hands were shaking as he pulled the car out and told me to shut the passenger door. I kept looking behind wondering where the man had come from. As we drove towards home, I was absolutely terrified. Although, my father had threatened me in the past, this was the first occasion that he had actually tried to kill me. I was glad when I reached home safe and alive. My father sat in the car for a couple for minutes before he allowed me to go into the house. When I entered the house I went upstairs to my bedroom. I stared at the walls for minutes. Shortly afterwards, I heard my father entering the house. After a few minutes, I heard him going into his bedroom. Moments later, I went downstairs and stepped into a cold shower. I noticed I had been bleeding. I scrubbed my body with Dettol.

When I awoke the following morning, I heard my mother and brother talking downstairs. Shortly afterwards, they left the house. I crept downstairs, hoping that my father wouldn't hear me. When I entered the kitchen, I felt cold and tired in the morning due to a lack of sleep and didn't eat any breakfast. Shortly afterwards, I went into the bathroom. Unfortunately, my father heard me washing myself in the bathroom and called me into his bedroom. When I entered his bedroom, he told me to put a bright face on at my job and promised that he would never touch me again. I didn't listen to him. I was thinking of who to contact and report what had happened the previous night. (I was later to discover at my father's trial that my sister had overheard some of the comments my father had made to me that morning.) When he had finished threatening me, I left for work.

When I arrived in work, one of my work colleagues commented that I looked very pale. At 10am I had a 15 minute work break. I rushed down to the coin telephone box across the road from my workplace, rang the operator and asked her for the number of the Galway Rape Crisis Centre. She accidentally put me through to the Cork centre. I spoke to a counsellor from the Cork centre and told her that I had been raped by my father and that I was afraid to go home. She told me that I should contact the Galway centre. I said I would and returned to work. As I put my uniform on, a work colleague grabbed me and asked me if there was something bothering me. I told her that there wasn't. She told me there was and said that I was usually joking with my work colleagues and laughing and that over the past two days I seemed very distant. She said that she suspected that my father had something to do with my state of mind and asked me if my father had hurt me in some way. I told her that he had and burst into tears and ran into the toilet and got physically sick. She asked me if I would mind if she asked a work colleague what to do. She called her over and her friend cried and comforted me.

When our supervisor spotted us, she couldn't understand why there were two girls around me in the cloakroom. When we returned to work, my work colleagues told me not to worry and that they would help.

I WOKE UP ON A COLD FLOOR

It wasn't long before lunch I collapsed and a Doctor from Spiddal was called. When I came to, all my work colleagues were gathered around me in a circle. The Doctor took me into a private room and told me that I should contact my GP urgently as he would have all my medical records. The Doctor asked me if I had eaten recently? I told her that I hadn't eaten anything for breakfast that morning. I explained to her that I was having severe chest pains. As soon as I came out of the room, the Manager asked me how I was. I told him that the Doctor suggested that I see my own GP. He told me that he would take me to my GP immediately. I told him that it was in Carna, nearly 60 miles away. He told me not to worry as he travelled from Tipperary to work every morning. As soon as I arrived in the clinic in Carna, a Doctor came out and called me into his office. My own Doctor was on holidays. He told me the last time he had seen me was when I was having difficulties eating and that he had helped me gain back my strength with vitamin drinks. I told him that I had collapsed in work and that I had severe chest pains. He noticed I was very anxious. After he had examined me, he told me to come back to him the next day if my symptoms persisted.

The following day, I told my mother that I was suffering with severe chest pains and that my mouth had gone purple. My mother was shocked when she saw the colour of my lips. She drove down to the village to a public phone and I rang the Doctor in Carna and told him that my condition seemed to be getting worse. As soon as I got off the phone, I told my mother that the Doctor had told me that I should come to him immediately and if necessary he would drive from Carna to our home in Carraroe. My mother told me that we had to go home and get my clothes in case the Doctor sent me to Hospital. I told her not to bother going home. I was afraid that my father would convince her not to travel to my GP in Carna. Also, I wanted to tell my mother what had happened to me on our journey in the car. I was hoping that I would be on my own with her. She insisted we go home in the car to collect my clothes.

As soon as we walked in the door, my father immediately asked my mother what the Doctor had said. My mother told him that the Doctor suggested I should see him straight away. My father told my mother that he would be happy to drive all the way to Carna. I asked my mother in his presence to come with me. My father wasn't too pleased. He pretended that he was concerned that my mother might have been too tired to drive such a long distance. Eventually, the three of us headed off in the car. On the journey, my father kept cracking jokes. He tried his best to put a smile on my face. Forty minutes later, we arrived at the clinic in Carna. The Doctor called me in immediately. He told me to sit up on the couch and examined my tummy. I repeated the same story about the chest pains to him. As he examined me, he said "Forgive me for saying this but you have the same symptoms as somebody who has suffered some form of abuse." For the first time since the abuse began, a sense of relief engulfed me. I broke down in tears. I told the Doctor that I had waited for somebody to say this all my life. I told him I couldn't come out with the words clearly. He was shocked when I explained to him how my father had raped and tried to strangle me two nights before that. He stood up, went over to the window and pulled up the blinds. He then asked me if both my parents were in the car? I told him that both my parents had brought me to the clinic. When he had finished examining me, the Doctor told me to return to my parents car and tell them that he was having me admitted to Galway Hospital. Before I left the clinic, the Doctor rang Galway Hospital and informed them that I was to be admitted that evening.

While I was in Hospital, two agents from the social services visited me and told me that they would have to inform my mother what had happened to me. As soon as I gave my details to the social services officers, one of the officer's reminded me that she had dealt with my mother years ago. She told me that my father had beaten my mother on more than one occasion and that she had suggested to my mother to move to Galway city and to leave her violent husband. Before she left, she told me that she was going to inform my mother on Friday what had happened to me. At the time, I wondered how my mother would react on hearing the news as my father had told me on more than one occasion that she would take it badly and probably end up having a heart attack. For the following two days, I was extremely anxious wondering how things were going to pan out.

On Friday morning, my mother received a letter at home asking her to attend an appointment in Carraroe Health Centre at 2pm. My mother immediately told my father. My father obviously realised something had happened and that the cat was probably out of the bag. He made an excuse to my mother that he had to collect my sister. When my mother said that it was too early to collect her, he told my mother that he needed to drop down to the local shop to buy some cigarettes. My father left the house.

Shortly afterwards, as I was heading towards the x-ray room in a wheelchair to have x-rays taken of my chest and abdomen, a nurse approached and told the porter who was pushing me to bring me over to the nurses office as there was somebody on the phone wishing to speak to me. The porter stopped the wheelchair outside the nurses office and the call was transferred to the corridor phone. I immediately recognised my father's voice on the other end of the line. My father told me that the social services had contacted my mother and wanted to see her that afternoon in the local Health Centre. He asked me if I had opened my mouth. I told him that I had. He started making threats immediately. I started crying. He warned me to keep my mouth shut and that if anything happened to him that I would suffer. He mentioned some of the nastier things he had done over the years, specifically referring to an incident where he claimed to have blown up a sergeant's house approximately forty miles from our home. He then threatened to kill me. I dropped the phone. The porter saw me in a distressed state and asked me if everything was ok. A few of the nurses approached and asked me if everything was ok. I looked up at them and told them that my father had been on the phone threatening me. They told me not to worry. The porter then wheeled me down to the x-ray room for my x-rays.

That afternoon, I phoned the social services. I asked how my mother had taken the news. They told me that she was upset but had taken the news as well as could be expected. The social worker told me that my mother was on my side. In the meantime, my father had disappeared. While my mother was attending her appointment with the social worker, my father had collected some of his clothes and belongings and had driven off in the car. My younger brother told me that my father shook his hand and told him that he never did anything on him. My brother got on his bike and left the house. He was on his way down the road when he saw my mother approaching him in the car. He asked her what was going on? My mother told my younger brother that she hoped my father had left and that my father had done something terrible. As all this unfolded, I waited anxiously in my hospital room. I would walk as far as the church hospital, downstairs, and say a couple of prayers and return to my room. My mother phoned me that evening and told me that she had been told about what had happened. As Galway Hospital was 25 miles away from our home, she told me that she wouldn't be able to visit that evening but would visit me the following day. She told me not to worry about my father. She suspected that he had taken the boat to England. I wondered how he managed to leave for England in such a short space of time. At this juncture, my mother suggested not to press charges against my father and that if he had left the country that I would never have to see him again. That afternoon, my younger sister explained to me over the phone that my father had told my mother not to listen to whatever I said. My father told her that I was a liar.

Later that evening, as I walked down the hospital corridor, I spotted my father standing at a radiator in the hall, beside the nurses office. He was wearing a long blue raincoat. I was shivering when I saw him standing there, unshaven. He approached me and began to speak. He told me that he hadn't moved to England. He told me that if I made any statements to the police that he would strangle me. Suddenly, I spotted my elder brother, Tony and my cousin approaching. I greeted my brother and cousin. My cousin immediately sensed there was tension between my father and I. My brother told me that mam had telephoned him and told him that my father had moved out. Tony was studying in Galway and had no idea what had taken place in the family home during his absence. When Tony asked me what was happening, I told him to contact my mother and not to listen to my father. I told him that I didn't want to upset him. He consented and no longer asked any further questions on the matter. When my brother was finished chatting to me, my father offered him a lift home. I was unhappy to see my brother leaving with him. Before my father left, he told me to think long and hard about what he had said. I knew my father would have little difficulty manipulating my brother. I was upset and didn't know what to do after being threatened by my father on the corridor of the hospital.

The following day, my mother and four siblings visited me in hospital. My mother leaned over the bed and gave me a hug. She told me that she was sorry to hear what had happened to me. She sensed that I was on edge and she had learned from the social services that I had expressed concerns about returning home. My family stood in front of me and promised that they would support me, no matter what. My family left after a couple of hours.

Later that afternoon, I received a telephone call from my Tony telling me that the story had spread around our village. He told me that the girl that I had first confided in was upset and had told some of my work colleagues why I had fainted. Tony told me that our cousin heard her and that he went back to my brother with the story. I was livid when I discovered that Tony had told people in the locality that I was a little confused. Tony had decided to tell people that my father had an affair with a lady behind my mother's back and that I had been mistaken telling the social worker that I had been raped. I could not believe what Tony was telling me over the phone. I told him that people would think that I was a liar. As I lay helpless in a hospital bed, Tony was telling everyone that I was inventing stories. My brother seemed to be more concerned about public opinion or the shame involved rather than the hurt I had suffered. His main concern was that the story wouldn't become public knowledge. His hope was that it could be kept quiet. Later that day, I received another telephone call from my father threatening me again. That evening, between

9 and 10 o'clock, as I was walking from my room towards the toilet, a drip hanging out of my arm, my father appeared out of nowhere and pushed me violently into the toilet. As soon as he realised we were alone in the toilet, he began to unbuckle his trouser belt and told me that he was going to rape me again. He told me, "I must do this to you again because the story is out now." I started screaming hysterically. My screams appeared to unnerve him. He pulled his trousers up and fastened his belt and ran. Despite my screams, no member of the medical staff came to my assistance. As I walked out of the toilet, I spotted my father rushing down the corridor towards an exit door. I was surprised to see him move so quickly for a man who was apparently suffering from high blood pressure. I approached the nurses office. It was empty. I returned to my hospital room and immediately pressed the nurses bell. I was disorientated and began searching under my bed and in my wardrobe to ensure my father wasn't hiding there. I was frightened and felt unsafe in my hospital room. I was extremely anxious. After what seemed like an age, a nurse appeared. I asked her why no one had come to my aid and had they not heard my screams. I told the nurse that my father had tried to rape me in the toilet. She apologised. A student nurse came in to chat with me afterwards.

Later that evening, my mother phoned me. I told my mother what had happened. She told me that she couldn't believe that my father had attempted to do this again. I told her that I felt unsafe in the hospital.

The following week, I received a call from my brother and sister informing me that my father had signed himself into a psychiatric ward in the same hospital that I had been admitted to (truth is sometimes stranger than fiction) I felt threatened.

I immediately informed all the nursing staff . I told them that I was extremely nervous after hearing that my father was a "patient" in the same hospital. Again, the nursing staff reassured me. I believe he had himself admitted in case I pressed charges and was going to pretend that he was mentally unstable. I was at my wits end knowing this man was intent on doing me some harm. One afternoon, my mother visited me and told me that she had visited my father in the psychiatric ward.

Two days later, my father appeared on my ward dressed in pyjamas. He was accompanied by my brother Tony. I felt frightened as they approached. My brother told me that he had informed everybody that my father was having an affair and that rumours that I had been sexually abused were nonsense. My father told me in no uncertain terms that this was the story that the entire family would be sticking to. My brother looked at me and told me not to press the nurses bell. My father was well able to pretend that he was depressed in front of my brother. He knew how to manipulate my brother and isolate him from the rest of the family. Before my father left he threatened me again and told me that I had better go along with the story that my brother was telling everybody. Later that week I learnt that my mother had signed him out. I told her that I heard about her signing him out. My mother told me that my eldest brother put pressure on her to get him out as the Doctors had been less than sympathetic towards him.

When I returned home from hospital, I discovered that Tony was now living with my father and uncle in Galway city. Tony had apparently moved out of our house the day after my had father left. He told my mother that he had sympathy for my father and that my father had told him that he was considering suicide. He told my mother that things were very hard on my father and that my father was coughing up blood and suffering from high blood pressure. Two days later, my father and Tony arrived outside our house. Tony got out of the car and came into the house. Tony told my mother that he missed her and the home made bread that she used to bake and that he was now staying with his father in Galway city. When Tony asked my mother if my father could come in, I told my brother that I would call the police if my father approached the hall door. He promised me that he wouldn't let him in. After chatting to my mother for about 30 minutes, my brother left.

At the time, I wasn't able to return to work. I missed the people that I worked with as they were great fun. As I sat at home, I thought about the good times I used to have with them. I missed the stories they used to tell. I had to leave all that behind while I was trying to recover. Tension began to rise between my mother and I. We weren't getting on. I complained to my mother that I didn't want my father to be entering the property at all.

One night, as I lay awake in bed, I heard the sound of a car engine coming up the driveway. I jumped out of bed quickly, looked out the window and noticed the person was driving very slowly, with the car headlights on. I immediately sensed it was my father. I left the light off in the bedroom and told my mother downstairs to remain calm. I knew that she would have heard the car coming before I had. She told me that it was going to be ok and to stay in bed. I didn't. Strangely it wasn't the same car that my father owned. It was a Peugeot. I opened up the drawer in the bedroom and grabbed the little red pocket knife that I had bought in Lourdes. I thought about the comment my father had made 3 weeks prior to that, when he had tried to choke me to death, 'I have to kill the evidence in case you ever come forward." I sat on top of the stairway in silence waiting for a knock on the door. I looked through the window at the side of the stairway to see if I could spot him. He had parked the car beside an old shed and was sitting alone in the dark. As I watched him, I noticed that he would start the car and drive around the house from time to time to try and scare us. My sisters were in bed. I don't really remember if they heard him that night. I stood there and kept staring out at the car. Instinctively, I knew he was sitting there wondering what to do next. I sat on top of the stairway looking out the window until the car pulled off. I noticed that my mother was afraid wondering what he was going to do. My younger brother wasn't home that night. He was staying in Maamcross, the place where he worked. I was under the impression that Niall had ongoing contact with my father. The following morning, my mother and I had a conversation about my father's behaviour of the previous night. My mother commented that my father was driving someone else's car.

My younger brother came home for the weekend. He told us that he had work commitments and was unable to visit as often as he would like. He also told us that he wouldn't have any contact with my father over what had happened. He told my mother and I that my father had tried to contact him at his workplace. He told us that he made himself unavailable whenever my father showed up. I was becoming suspicious that his father was in contact with him. My friends told me that my father and my eldest brother would show up in Maamcross and collect my younger brother. My younger brother gave out to me in front of my family. I knew he was doing it for his father's benefit. My father had dropped off my eldest brother for a short period of time to visit my mother. That afternoon, my younger brother hit me on the nose. He told me that he had hit me because the story regarding the abuse had become public. He told me that I shouldn't have told anybody about the abuse and that the family would be forever shamed. At the time, I was unable to retaliate. My arms were still bruised after the drip and I was extremely weak. As I touched my nose, I noticed that there was blood dripping from my nose. My brother empathised with his father who had kicked and beaten him as a child (some people can love their abusers....). My younger sister told my brothers that it was true what had happened to me. My brothers sat on the bed and laughed and made what they presumed were funny comments about me being raped by my father. I explained to my brother that the story my father had told him about being suicidal, coughing up blood or chest pains were the same stories that he had told me after raping me. I told my brother that my father was manipulating him and trying to turn my family against me. I realised that Tony was looking in the opposite direction as I attempted to explain my father's manipulative behaviour. However, I also realised that it was time for me to heal. Around them I couldn't see that happening. In a way, I was glad Tony was no longer living with us as he hadn't proved to me in any way that he was a man, as he never stood up to his father and confronted him about what he had done to me.

Niall stood by us for a while. After three months, he moved away with his father and Tony. Niall wasn't too happy to move to a different house. I remember one day around the month of September or October, Niall tried to stop an argument between my mother and I. After the argument, I left the house in anger and went back the road to the sea. I ran up to the rock and was approaching the oncoming tide when my brother walked right up behind me and grabbed my arm. He had a concerned look on his face and tried to convince me that things weren't as bad as they seemed and that my situation would improve. He asked me to return to the house and pleaded with me not to do anything drastic. He was shocked to see that my face was red from crying. He promised me while he would be around that they wouldn't argue with me. I screamed and told him to move away and told him that there was no need for him to try and save me. He began to cry and grabbed my arm and helped me climb back up the rocks. As soon as we returned to our house, Niall started to remonstrate with my mother and told my mother that I needed her full support.

At the time, I had great difficulty reconciling myself to the fact that I had lost my elder brother whom I adored. I had to reconcile myself to the fact that my eldest brother had decided to take my father's side in this case. Fortunately, at this juncture I had the support of my younger brother, not realising there was more heartache on the way. As well as being physically abused by my father, it was also evident that

I had been emotionally traumatised. Physically, my father had violated me. However, due to this abuse he also managed to emotionally scar me. At that time, I considered suicide the only viable solution to my dilemma. However, something inside kept me going and somehow I managed to resist the constant feeling that my life had no value. It wasn't easy for me at the beginning when neighbours were throwing their eye wondering if I was telling the truth. May god forgive those who thought I was telling lies.

I tried to dress nicely and to appear to be happy in front of others. However, I was living a lie, suffering in silence. I believe that all people can dress well if they so wish. It is merely an image and doesn't portray the inner being. I used to change my image all the time. I guess that was a way of discovering my inner-self. At the time, I had little reason to be happy with my appearance. My father had managed over a period of time to convince me that I was an unattractive human being of little value. My sisters, on occasion, were guilty of the same behaviour.

One night, I awoke to hear loud banging on our front door. My mother got out of bed in her dressing gown. I got out of bed and listened at the side of the stairs and spotted Tony and my father entering the house. They both were drunk and began interrogating my mother. She was sitting on the couch and I heard her fixing the turf in the fire a few times with the tongs. A few nights after that, my father returned with my brother. I opened the door and told my brother that if he wanted to visit us not to bring his father with him. I told my brother that if my father entered the premises again that I would contact the Police and press charges. My brother entered the house and spoke to my mother. Tony told my mother that my father wanted to speak to her to straighten things out. He persuaded my mother to speak to my father. My mother went out and spoke to my father. While my mother was outside speaking with my father, my brother told me that he wanted to get our parents back together. I told him that I would never live under the same roof as my father. He told me that my father suggested that he would take care of my mother and two sisters. I became very angry and told my brother that I would under no circumstances allow my father to remain under the same roof as my two younger sisters. I told my brother that I felt that my sisters wouldn't be safe under the same roof as my father. My mother returned to the house and told me that she was going out with my father for dinner in Clifden and that he was trying to get things back to normal between them. I was extremely angry and told my mother that she was breaking a promise that she had made to me. I was also very annoyed with Tony. My brother wanted our neighbours to see my father accepted back into the family. Tony wanted to create the impression that everything was fine in our family and the allegations of abuse were untrue. My mother returned home later that night safe and sound. I was disgusted when I discovered the following morning that my father had slept with my mother that night. That morning, I saw my mother washing clothes in the bathroom. She was tearful when I approached her. She told me that my father had suggested that she was having an affair with her own father. My father told Tony that every man in the village was abusing their daughters and that such behaviour was quite common. Sadly, my brother believed him. When I spotted my father coming out of my mother's room, I refused to speak to him. He made some comment about my bag trying to make conversation. I didn't say a word to him. He sat at the kitchen table apparently fixing the kettle. He told my younger brother Niall that a fuse had blown in it. He opened the wires and did something to them. He put the fuses cross ways thinking that I was the one who was going to plug it in again. He had another thing coming. When my father and brother had left, Niall checked the plug. Niall told mam that we were lucky that he had checked the plug.

Niall suggested that my father tried to cross the wires in the plug to try and create an explosion.

Later that morning, I heard someone banging on our front door. As I lay in the bed, I realised that my younger brother wasn't at home to answer it. I thought mam was sleeping. I decided to look out the window and see if I could find out who was there before I opened the door. I dressed and went downstairs and opened the door halfway. It was my elder brother. He asked if mam was in? I told him that I was only out of bed. He wanted me to check her bedroom. I checked her room, but couldn't find her there. He told me not to worry as he had a good idea where she might be. As he left, I warned him not to return to the house with my father. I watched my father and brother drive off in the direction of my grandfather's house. I spotted my brother in the distance stopping the car outside my grandfather's house. My brother got out of the car and knocked on my grandfather's door. Initially there was no response. He then knocked on one of the windows. Suddenly the front door opened. My grandfather stood there and asked my brother what he wanted. My brother asked him if my mother was there. My grandfather told my brother that she was taking a bath. My mother then came to the door, dressed in a green dressing gown. My father got out of the car and began to row with my mother. He asked her why she couldn't take a bath in her own home. My father then suggested that my mother was having an affair with her own father. My mother blushed. My father and brother got back into the car and approached our house. They stopped the car outside our house. My brother got out, walked towards me and told me that our mother was having an affair with her father. I told him that his father was putting sick thoughts in his head and that I didn't believe him. I told him to leave and take our father with him.

My father and brother arrived back at the house two days later. My mother opened the door to them. They told my mother that they had left a letter in my Grandfathers letterbox telling him to stay away from my mother. My father told my mother that her father was interfering with their marriage. My mother told my father that he was sick and that nothing was going on between her and her father. My father and brother left. Later that afternoon, my mother visited her father. Her father showed her the letter that my father had written and signed. My mother told me later that evening that her father was very upset when he received the letter. He also told my mother that he was very upset when he heard that the man she had married had sexually interfered with one of his grandchildren. He told my mother to get as far away from him as quickly as possible.

That weekend, I dropped into our local Hotel. In the hotel, I overheard people discussing details of my story. Sadly, the story was being embellished all the time. It was now common knowledge in the locality that my father had sexually abused me. A man told me in the Hotel that he had heard that I had given birth while I was in hospital. I told him that people were embellishing the story and that I did not in fact have a child. I mentioned to him that some of my work colleagues had visited me in the hospital and had suggested that I had been beaten when they noticed bruising on my arm. I told him that it was the result of the drip placed in my arm.

Three months passed. One morning, my mother's brother arrived and began shifting all our furniture out of the house. I asked my mother what was happening. My mother told me that we were going to live with her father. I was distraught. I had little trust in men and no trust in elderly men. I begged my mother not to bring us to her father's house. I told her that for the first time in years that I had a sense of peace. However, my mother was not to be swayed. By the afternoon, all our furniture and belongings were in my grandfather's house. I had little affection for this man who had intermittently shown my mother signs of paternal love. Niall stayed with us every weekend.

One night, I heard a car pulling up outside my grandfather's house. My grandfather got out of bed and went down to investigate what was happening. Before he opened the front door the car sped away. A white bag had been left beside the front door. We later discovered that the white powder contained in the bag was for poisoning animals. This incident made my mind up for me. I was convinced that my father and probably my eldest brother had left the bag outside my grandfather's door. I discussed the situation with my mother. Although I had no desire to prosecute my father (even though he had ruined my childhood) my mother and I decided it was time for me to press charges against him. Initially, I sat at home and wrote 30 pages on the history of my abuse. This was a very painful exercise. I had to relive many negative experiences that I wished to forget. I had to list the locations where my father had raped me and to some degree describe the type of abuse that had taken place. My mother and I subsequently contacted the Garda in Salthill, Co. Galway.

PATRICK NAUGHTON'S
FIRST ARREST

The police were very helpful and arranged a time for me to make a statement. I found the experience very embarrassing. At home, the relationship between my younger brother and the rest of the family began to deteriorate. Every time Niall visited us, he would argue incessantly with my mother. Unknown to us, my younger brother was associating with my father and elder brother. Sadly, he seemed to have taken the side of his father in this dispute. My father was arrested in Galway and taken to the local police station. Initially he refused to answer any questions that the Police asked. Ultimately, he began to communicate, reluctantly. He denied everything and called me a liar. He tried to confuse the police and mentioned names of people who had long since passed on. The police gradually became exasperated with his behaviour. They released him after several hours of questioning. A policewoman visited me a week later. She told me that my father had been very unhelpful and had wasted the time of the police officers who had questioned him. I told her that I wanted to pursue the charges that I had made.

A week later, I arrived home from Galway city to discover that Niall had moved out. There had been an argument between himself and my grandfather. I discovered that Niall was working in a bar in Galway. I spoke to Niall and he told me that his aunt had managed to source an apartment for him and was financially supporting him until he could support himself. I asked my brother to have as little contact with my father as he possibly could. He promised that he would have nothing to do with my father and hated him for what he had done to me. Subsequently, I discovered that my younger brother had decided, like my elder brother, to shack up with my father. I was very disappointed on hearing this news.

A warrant had been issued for my father's re-arrest. The police were looking for him again. A file was sent to the DPP in relation to my allegations. My father and elder brother were nowhere to be found. I began to suspect that my father had left the country. Two weeks passed. One evening we received a phone call at home. My mother answered the phone. My elder brother was on the other end of the line. He told her that he had fallen down a flight of stairs in Corbett's Court, while working as a security officer and was currently lying in a bed in Merlin Park hospital. When asked about his father my brother told my mother that he had no contact with our father and no idea of my father's current whereabouts. However, I was not convinced that my brother had no direct contact with my father. My mother immediately dropped the phone, gathered my two sisters and drove in to Galway to visit my brother in hospital. Five minutes after my mother arrived in the hospital, my father arrived in with my younger brother. My parents spoke for several minutes. My mother left with her two daughters in tow. My father tried to follow my mother out of the hospital, however my mother was no longer interested in hearing his lies. My brother phoned from the hospital that night and spoke to my mother. He told my mother that he had no idea that my father would be visiting him at the same time. He told my mother that he would be discharged from the hospital in a couple of days. Then my brother asked to speak to me. He told me that he was sorry that he hadn't been more supportive of me. Strangely, I thought I heard my father's voice in the background speaking to my brother. I could hear my father giving my brother directions. My father was telling my brother to try and persuade me to visit him in the hospital alone. I believed that my brother was trying to set a trap for me (at this stage I was entitled to be extremely careful when having dealings with members of my family). From that day on, I found it very difficult to trust anybody.

When my mother returned home, she rang the police station in Salthill and informed the officer on duty that she had encountered my father in the hospital. The following day, my father was re-arrested while driving to Merlin Park to give my brother some clothes.

Later that evening, Tony telephoned my mother and asked my mother why she had informed on my father. My mother told my brother that it was the right thing to do. The police questioned my father for a second time. My father again denied everything and was released later that evening. Tony was annoyed. He had been waiting for his father to bring his clothes into the hospital for him. Tony telephoned my mother and told her that it was wrong to arrest his father and he didn't want to give any information on where my father was currently living.

My family commented to me that people were saying this and that about what they thought had happened. My mother and sisters told me that a lady from our neighbourhood told them that I had made allegations against my father because he wouldn't let me go to the local disco with my friends. I was very hurt when I overheard my mother's aunt saying that I could have dressed to seduce my father. I was very hurt and disgusted when my younger sister told me that it was only stupid people who were raped. I knew that she was unaware that I had saved both my sisters childhoods. Every time I went to Galway in the car I was reminded of the locations where I was abused, including the lake in Tully. I hated seeing that place. All the painful memories would flood back into my mind.

Shortly afterwards, I had my first real boyfriend. He lived outside Galway city and used to bring me out in his hometown. He was a very nice person. He treated me well. He used to buy me lovely gifts and bring me out to clubs in Galway city. Six months into the relationship, I decided to put an end to it as I had no intention of settling in Galway. I needed my freedom and I was terrified of anyone who wanted to possess me. I wanted to travel and hopefully visit the United States one day. He was heartbroken when the relationship ended, but what could I do.

One day, Grainne returned home from school. She went to her bedroom without communicating with anyone. This was very unusual behaviour for my sister. I followed her into her bedroom but found it very difficult to try and get information out of her about what was bothering her. Eventually, she told me that she had been bullied at school. I was upset to hear that. It reminded me of when I was her age. The following day I spotted the girl who had bullied my sister. She was with two of her friends and was walking in the direction of Doilin Beach. I approached her and told her not to be picking on my younger sister or she would have me to deal with. She apologised and said that it wouldn't happen again. After that the situation in school improved for my 13 year old sister.

On another occasion, my other sister got in trouble in school over one of my father's family. The girl she had the problem with was my father's sister's daughter. We weren't on good terms with his family. The teacher had given her pages to pass around in class. My sister told me that her cousin had thrown the pages on her desk and not placed them neatly like she had done for all the other students. My sister slapped her across the face outside the school. Our local priest spotted my sister slapping her cousin and remonstrated with her regarding her behaviour. My sister knew that my father's sister would send the police to our house and probably have my sister charged if it was possible.

A policeman arrived at our house the next morning. He told my mother that he would be questioning my sister at the school. I told him that it wouldn't be necessary to speak to my sister in the school as it would embarrass her. I told the Police officer that my sister was very sorry for what had happened and that she had promised that nothing like this would happen again.

During the Summer, I started working with my mother in Spiddal in the evenings. My father's sister was working there at the time. She was the lady that sent the police to our house in relation to my sister. One day, there was only my father's sister and I in the cloakroom. We were looking in opposite directions. I turned around when I noticed that she wouldn't talk to me. I told her that it was time to cut the bull.

I asked her why she wouldn't speak to me. I told her that I had heard that some of my father's relations had alleged that I was telling lies and that my father had in fact never touched me. She told me that she had never called me a liar in public and that if her brother had in fact committed any form of abuse that she hoped that he would be sent to jail for a very long time. My friends had told me that my father's other sister was telling my neighbours that the allegations I had made against my father were false and that I would be proved to be a liar.

One day, as I entered the sitting room, I heard my two younger sisters arguing over what they were going to watch on Television. My younger sister, Grainne, wanted to watch the news. My youngest sister, Aoifa, wanted to watch her music video. I told my youngest sister to switch off the music video and let my other sister watch the news and that when the news was over that she could put her music video back on. My two sisters began to argue again. As I tried to intervene, my youngest sister threw a glass of coke in my face. It splashed in my eyes and I was blinded for a couple of seconds. When I regained my sight, I slapped her across the face. She screamed and called my Grandfather. My grandfather and mother entered the sitting room. My youngest sister told them that I was crazy and had slapped her across the face. My grandfather clenched his fist. I began to cry. I told my grandfather and mother that my sister had thrown a glass of coke in my face. I looked in the direction of my other sister, looking for her support. However, she remained silent. My grandfather told me to keep my hands to myself and left the room. I looked in the direction of my other sister and asked her why she hadn't spoken when my grandfather and mother entered the room. She mumbled something and left the room sheepishly.

One day, I recall my sister was playing her music very loudly. My grandfather gave out to her. He walked upstairs and pulled the plug from the wall. As he pulled the plug from the wall, the plug hit a bedside lamp and shattered the glass. My sister screamed and said that the lamp was a present my younger brother had bought for her when he used to live with us. I spoke to my mother about the incident. Our conversation became heated and my mother lost her temper. My mother grabbed me by the hair and kept thumping my head on the bed. My two sisters ran into the room and told my mother to stop and not to suffocate me. I had a severe headache after she pulled my hair. After this incident I was crying and left the room. I left the room in anger. My mother went downstairs to continue chatting with my grandfather. It was evident that my grandfather was unused to such family squabbles. At the time, I was having constant rows with my mother. When I attended counselling during the week, I told the counsellor of the constant rows I was having with my family. My counselling sessions began to focus more on the ongoing rows I was having with my family, moreover than the sexual abuse I had experienced.

LOURDES

My mother arranged for me to go with a group to Lourdes. We flew from Shannon airport and arrived in France on a warm Summer morning and a coach brought us to the hotel where we were staying. When I walked to the grotto later that afternoon, the area was crowded with people. I returned to my hotel and had a nap. When I returned later that evening, there were far fewer people there. I felt at ease. I felt it was a very spiritual place where a person could reflect. As I sat on a wall, I stared at the sparkling candles and for the first time in ages felt at peace with myself. When I returned to my hotel room, I discovered that an elderly lady was sharing the room with me. At first, I felt uncomfortable. However, as I chatted to the elderly woman I felt totally at ease. The lady told me that she was from Loughrea, a town 40 miles from where I lived in Galway. She told me that she came to Lourdes as often as she could as she found the experience uplifting. As I jumped into bed, I spotted the elderly lady undressing and placing a navy nun's uniform on the chair beside her bed. I wondered what type of conversations I would have with a nun the following day. I decided immediately that I would agree with anything she had to say on religious matters.

The following morning as we chatted over breakfast, I began to develop a sincere affection for this elderly woman. She asked me to attend mass with her. As I walked around the grotto with her, I was shocked when she told me that it was very hard on her living without her husband. I told her that I had seen her nun's uniform and I thought that nuns didn't marry. She smiled and told me that she had left the nuns' order years ago and that she only wore the uniform whenever she visited Lourdes. She was a very interesting human being and excellent company. She told me that when she was young she wanted to explore life and that she didn't want to feel trapped rushing to the church all the time. When we reached the grotto, I told her that I wasn't fond of walking around the grotto during the day. However, I told her that I loved sitting there at night looking up at the stars and watching the candles sparkle. I felt a deeper connection at night sitting there on my own. I spent the following day walking around looking at souvenirs with some ladies from Kinnvarra, my original home town.

The next day, I decided to go on a day trip to Paris. I enjoyed it. I liked the French people. They were very friendly. There were a few girls there from Germany t who tried to speak English to me. When I returned to Lourdes, I spent the evening in the Hotel Solitude that was located within walking distance of my own Hotel. There was a singing competition in the hotel that evening. I sang with a group of people and also sang a song on my own. There was a priest from Oughterard there. He was a very talented singer. He was also an excellent raconteur and he kept the entire company amused with his amusing stories.

I spent the night before returning home packing my suitcase in my hotel room. When I had finished packing my bags, I decided to visit the grotto for the last time. As I walked towards the elevator, I fainted in the hallway. When I awoke, I noticed one of the Hotel porters checking through one of my suitcases. The porter had gone to my room and brought all my luggage. The Hotel staff were under the impression that

I may have been a diabetic and were checking my luggage to see if I had any medication that may have been of assistance. As soon as they realised that I was awake, they told me that I had to go to casualty. Initially, I told them there was nothing wrong with me and that I had no desire to go to casualty. However they told me it was hotel policy and eventually I relented. They kept me on a drip in casualty overnight. I was giddy in hospital and wanted to leave. The Doctor wanted to ensure that I would be all right and feeling better before he discharged me. Finally, the hotel arranged for me to go on an earlier flight the next morning. When I boarded the plane, the airhostess approached me and asked me if there was anything she could do for me. She told me that she had been told that I had been unwell and that if I felt unwell at anytime during the flight to call her immediately.

When I arrived in Galway, I said goodbye to my neighbours. My mother was waiting for me in the car park. My mother greeted our neighbours from the flight as they put their suitcases in their cars. They told her that I had fainted in the hotel. When I arrived home, I showed my sisters the pictures of Lourdes. When I lifted the souvenirs I had bought out of my travel case, my mother and sisters began to laugh.

They especially liked the little donkey, who spat fire from his rear end. When I finally emptied my case, Grainne asked me if I had brought back any religious souvenirs. I told her that I hadn't.

Weeks later, my mother got a wedding invitation from a relative in England. My mother, two sister and I headed off to London. On our way to my relations house, my mother noticed that some coloured men were staring at me. When I asked her why they were staring at me, she said it was because of my blonde hair. My mother told me that blonde coloured hair looked cheap. I told my mother that I would darken my hair that evening. When I returned to my cousin's house that night, I put a darker dye in my hair. The following morning, when my mother, two sisters and I went to the bus stop, some coloured men kept looking at me. Apparently the colour of my hair made very little difference. My mother told me to ignore them. We had a good time at the wedding and danced all night.

When the Director of Public Prosecution released the file on my father's arrest, my father was nowhere to be found. I believe he was living with my two brothers in England at the time. The police seemed to be powerless and informed me that nothing could be done until my father returned to Ireland. I was upset and anxious thinking that he would never come back. I realised that my father was convinced that the Irish State would never prosecute him as he had been released on the two other occasions that he had been arrested. My father was under the impression that he was a free man. One evening, my father's brother approached my mother while she was having a quiet drink with her father in the pub and told her that he hoped that I wouldn't prosecute my father.

FEBRUARY 2001

In February 2001, my two younger sisters received a surprise telephone call from Tony. It had been a couple of years since we had heard a word from my brother. He told them that he was back in Ireland and that he wanted to arrange to meet them somewhere locally. Later that evening, my brother collected my two sisters from our house. As soon as they jumped in the car, my brother asked them if they would speak to their father if he returned to Ireland. They said they wouldn't know what to say to him. My brother then told them that he was taking them for a drive to one of his friend's. Before they left, my sisters ran back into the house and told my mother and I they were going for a drive with Tony. I told my sisters that I wouldn't allow them to go on their own. Initially, my brother dropped up to one of his friend's. He then drove towards my father's parents house in Kinvarra. I asked my brother where we were going. He told me that he was dropping up to see our grandparents. As we arrived at our grandparents house, my brother jumped out of the car and approached the front door of my grandparents house. Suddenly, my father appeared at the wall of the front garden. I was both surprised and frightened. I looked at my sisters and told them to remain calm. My father approached and sat on the passenger seat of the car. Tony returned and sat in the driver's seat while my father spoke to my sisters.

I gave Tony a strange look. My father looked at the house where we had lived until I was 16 and said that he was sad that he had ever sold the house as he had fond memories of the place. I told my brother that I wanted to return to Carraroe. My father told my sisters to keep in touch. As he got out of the car, I remained silent. My brother pointed to my father standing at the back of the house where we used to live saying that my father had lots of regrets. I told him that he didn't think hard enough before he raped me. My brother told me there was no need to bring that up and he changed the subject. As soon as he dropped us off at our home, my sisters ran into the house and told my mother that my father had come home for his birthday and that he was planning to have a meal with his parents in Furbo House to celebrate his birthday. My mother immediately phoned the police and informed the officer on duty that my father was back in the country. The policewoman made contact with the Carraroe police. They made arrangements to meet up in Casla to find my father's family home. My mother told me she had called the police. I told her that if my father realised that the police were after him that he would get on the first boat headed for England. I told my mother to tell the police not to send uniformed Gardai to any of my father's relatives houses, but to send plain clothes police officers if they wanted to catch him. My mother agreed with me. My mother told me that she would direct the police to my father's family home.

That night, I travelled with her to my father's house. The police came from Galway city and drove out to Kinnvarra. My mother and I were directing them from the front. We noticed my father's brother passing in the car. I was concerned in case he would turn back. Thankfully he didn't notice us at all. When we arrived at my father's parents house, 16 police officers jumped out of their police cars and surrounded the house. There would be no escape for my father this time. I went to the front door and called my brother out. I could hear several voices coming from within the house. My father's mother came out first and invited me into her home. I told her that I was in a hurry. Seconds later, my father stepped out of his parent's house and greeted me. Immediately, he sensed something. He rushed in the house again. At the time the police were hiding behind the wall next door to the house where I was brought up in. My mother was with them. They didn't recognise my father because he had his hair shaved off. My father called Tony and told him that I wanted to see him.

When my brother came to the door, I asked him if he would like to go for a drink. He told me that he was too tired and that he was going for a rest. As I turned, he said he would walk me to my mother's car. He then asked me who my mother was visiting in the locality. I told him that my mother was visiting the lady across the road from where we used to live. I was nervous and told him that there was no need for him to walk all the way down to the car. I knew that he would get a shock if he saw the police. Suddenly he spotted a man with a navy jacket. The man had the jacket zipped up which made it difficult for my brother to figure out who he was. He asked me was he my boyfriend? I remained calm. My brother stared at him standing at the back window of Granny's house. My brother asked him to approach the house and kept asking him what he was doing there. The policeman walked towards him slowly and pulled the zip down on his jacket and told him that he was a Garda. My brother screamed so loud that the neighbours heard him. My father emerged from the house and asked my brother if there was anything wrong. My brother tried to speak to him, but his lips couldn't move. He was in shock. My father kept calling his name. Then my grandparents emerged from the house. My father saw the young dark haired policeman approaching. He didn't know who he was. My grandfather asked him what he was doing on his premises. The policeman walked closer to my father and arrested him. My father was speechless. His parents paled as they saw the rest of the police officers streaming over the wall. My brother's voice had returned and he followed my father, who had now been handcuff ed, towards a police car. As my father sat in the back seat of the police car, Tony told him not to worry that he would bail him out the following morning. The police looked at my brother in surprise when they saw him placing his hands on his head screaming. Two days later, my father appeared before the Circuit Court in Galway city. My brother offered to post £10,000 bail which the judge accepted. I was disappointed when I was told that my father was to be released on temporary bail.

THE UNITED STATES

At home, my relationship with my mother and two sisters deteriorated. The arguments between my sisters and I became more heated and I felt that I could not rely on their support. Eventually, I decided it was time to move out and I ended up renting a house in Carraroe village with a relative of my mother's. I spent a couple of months there before I decided it was time to pack my bags and head off to the United States. My family was under the impression that I would be returning within a few weeks. As I packed my suitcases, I knew in my heart that it would be a long time before I saw Galway again. When I arrived in Boston, it felt like I had entered another world. My life blossomed. Before I knew it, I was working in a model agency during the day and taking care of an elderly lady at night. She was 102 years old and one of the happiest people I had ever met in my life. Over a period of months, she told me about her life and her husband whom she adored.

As I started to earn a living, I began to frequent some of the Irish bars in Boston, where most of the Irish-Americans hung out. One evening, I met an extremely attractive man in one of the Irish pubs. He was of Italian extraction and had a gorgeous face. My friend had introduced him to me. He invited me out to see the musical "Les Miserable" that was showing in Boston. I was thrilled. I couldn't wait to see him the next morning. I went to the pub where we were supposed to meet. I loved how he dressed. He generally wore a lovely black suit. He had spent years in drama school and like other actors had dreams of going to Hollywood. I was more attracted to him when I discovered that he was an animal lover.

Three months later, he asked me if he could move in with me. I was delighted. I sensed this was the man for me. He had a wonderful extrovert personality and I always had a great time when we went out. He knew that I used to travel regularly to New York City. When I went to his local pub with him, I found it funny when his pals asked me for a date. I recall one night when he went to the toilet, one of his pals suggested that I should go out with a real man. I was a little surprised as I had believed that this man was one of my boyfriend's best friends. When we left the pub I told my boyfriend about his friend. Initially, he disbelieved me. I then showed him the note. He immediately recognised his friend's handwriting. My boyfriend was surprised when he discovered that his pal had behaved in such a manner. On our way home, I reassured him that I had no interest in his friend's opinion. My boyfriend used to write me wonderful poems. Whenever I used to come home from my workplace I used to find notes on the bedroom floor with love hearts and poems.

At the time, I was very happy with my job and was now helping to arrange fashion shows. Every morning, I went to the gym and exercised for a couple of hours. My life was complete. However, fate was to intervene. One afternoon, I received a telephone call in work from my mother back in Ireland. She told me that my father's trial was coming up and that I would have to return to Ireland for it. I was in two minds. I was very busy with the job now and all aspects of my personal life were rosy. Returning to Ireland would only bring unwanted pain. As I spoke to my mother, part of me wanted to ensure my father was punished for what he had taken from me. Another part of my being was telling me to remain in America and to continue with the life I was gradually building for myself and to tell my mother that I had no interest in returning to Ireland to relive painful memories. Part of me didn't want to go through the ordeal of a trial. The thoughts of publicly discussing what had happened to me as a child repulsed me. The thoughts of strangers hearing how I had been violated repulsed me. Finally, I told my mother that I would think about it and call her back.

When I returned home that evening, my mother had left a message on my answering machine. It was the 13th of September 2001, 2 days after the World Trade Centre had been destroyed by two airplanes. When I had listened to my mother's message, I rang her immediately. My mother was now apparently concerned about my safety as I was constantly visiting New York. She also said that the Irish Police had contacted her and had told her that they would like to liaise with me before the trial began. As I spoke to my mother, my boyfriend overheard some of my comments and asked me why my mother was asking me to return home to Ireland. I told him that I was needed as a witness for a trial back in Ireland and that I had no option but to return. As I had not confided my family history to him, I found it difficult to provide him with a truthful response. I merely looked at him and told him that my mother needed me.

Seconds later, I heard my younger sister's voice on the phone. She told me that my mother was extremely upset and very anxious over the upcoming trial. I felt torn in two. I had managed to leave this hurtful situation and it seemed that fate was dragging me back. I asked my sister to hand the phone back to my mother. As soon as I heard my mother's voice on the other end of the other line, I told her how I felt. I told her that I had managed to rebuild my life and that I felt nothing but pain awaited me back in Ireland. My mother sympathized with me, but told me that if I ever wanted Justice and closure from this matter that I would have to face my father in court. Finally, I consented and told my mother that I would arrange my flights before the end of the week. As soon as I hung up the phone, I turned to my boyfriend and told him that I would have to return to Ireland within the next two weeks. I told him that as soon as I had finished with matters in Galway that I would return to him immediately. He looked at me quizzically and asked me if there was anything I wanted to tell him about. At the time, I was still extremely embarrassed about my past and had no intention of discussing this thorny issue with him. Later that evening, while I was discussing the matter with my boyfriend, I received a call from Noreen Feeney, a police officer from Galway. Noreen had been one of the officer's who had taken my original statement. Noreen told me that she had been speaking to my mother and asked me if I had any concerns about the trial. I told her that I was hesitant and had started a new life in Boston and was in two minds about returning home. I told her that I would ring my mother and let my mother know what I was going to do. An hour later, I received a second call from another police woman from Galway. She told me that it would be easier to prosecute my father if I returned home as soon as possible. Again, I told her that I was still in two minds and I asked her what would happen to me if I didn't return. She told me that the DPP would probably apply to have me subpoenaed. Slowly, I realised that I had no option but to return and hopefully finalise this matter.

The day after, I booked my flight for the following day. I rang my mother and told her when I would be arriving in Shannon airport. She told me that she would collect me. The following evening, I dropped down to the local pub to have a final a drink with some of the friends I had made in Boston. They all told me that they were sorry to hear that I was returning to Ireland but hoped that I would return as soon as possible. When I returned from the pub later that evening, I sat in my bedroom and lit some candles and prayed that justice would be done on my return to Ireland. The following morning, my boyfriend asked me how long I would be in Ireland and if I was intending to return to Boston. I told him that I had every intention of returning as soon as I had completed my business over there. Shortly afterwards, my pal Mohammed arrived, grabbed my bags and drove me to the airport. Three hours later, I was on a plane heading across the Atlantic Ocean.

"Patrick Naughton outside the Four Courts, Dublin, 2002"
Photo Courtesy of Maxwell Photography

"Junior Minister, Bobby Molloy T.D."
Picture Courtesy of RTE Productions

"The lonely by-lane where Patrick Naughton
attempted to strangle Barbara, June 1997"

CENTRAL CRIMINAL COURT - DUBLIN

When I arrived in Dublin Airport, my mother and two sisters were waiting for me. Initially they had difficulty recognising me due to the colour and length of my hair, but I recognised them immediately. My two sisters ran over and threw their arms around me, then grabbed my suitcases. My mother followed them over and game me a hug. On our way back to Galway in my mother's car, I told my sisters all about my experiences in America and about my current boyfriend. The subject of the trial was never raised.. When I arrived back in Galway, the place looked a lot smaller to me. For the next few days, I remained at home, feeding the ducks and hens. Over the next four weeks, the police constantly rang my mother to confirm details of the upcoming trial. They told my mother that they had arranged accommodation for my family and I in Dublin.

A week before the case, I decided to visit Galway city. Whilst in Galway city, I spotted my father's sister. She looked surprised to see me and ignored me as I passed her on the street. My mother had told me that she had spread rumours that I had told lies about the entire affair and that none of the allegations of sexual abuse were true and that there was no chance that I would return from America to give evidence against my father.

A day before the trial was due to begin, my mother, two sisters and a representative of the Galway Rape Crisis Centre and I headed for Dublin on the train. When we arrived at Heuston station, we took a cab to the hotel where we would be staying for the duration of the trial. That night, I headed to bed early. The following morning, I got dressed and prepared myself for the upcoming ordeal. At 10.30 am, my mother, two sisters and I left our hotel and headed to the Four Courts. As I entered the room where my case would be heard, cold shivers ran down my spine. Although I had wanted justice, the reality of what a court case would entail slowly began to dawn on me. I would have to give evidence in front of strangers and have to describe events in my life that I had done everything I possibly could to forget. As I sat in my seat, the judge entered the room. Everyone in the courtroom stood, like what happens in church when the priest enters. As I looked around the room, I spotted my father standing in the dock. A police officer stood right beside him. I noticed an elderly man with grey hair standing directly beneath my father. The woman from the Galway Rape Crisis Centre told me the man was an interpreter and that my father would be responding to all the questions he was asked in Irish. When I turned to my mother and told her what was happening, she merely smiled and told me not to worry. As I turned my head, I spotted Tony sitting at the back of the courtroom with my father's sister. Shortly afterwards, my barrister stood up and began detailing the history of the case. As he continued to read, I noticed that my father was staring at my mother and my two sisters. When my barrister had finished detailing the case, the judge adjourned the case until the following day. As I stood up and looked around the courtroom, Tony was nowhere to be seen. Moments later, my mother, two sisters and I left the court. Later that afternoon, I walked around Dublin with my mother and sisters. When

I returned to the hotel later that evening, I decided to take a bath. As I lay in the bath and wondered how the trial would go, I tried to recall some of the instances of abuse and how I would relate them to a packed courtroom. It seemed to be a daunting matter and I knew that I would have some difficulty as my memory of some of the instances was blurred. I had over a period of years tried to forget these experiences and I slowly realised that my mind had no wish to relive these matters. However, I no longer had a choice. Shortly afterwards, I heard someone banging on the door of my hotel room. I then heard my mother and sisters calling my name and asking me to open the door. I shouted back and told them that I was in the bath and would be with them shortly. As soon as I dressed and opened the door, they rushed in and told me that Tony was downstairs in the hotel bar. Although I had every wish to see my brother, something in the back of my mind told me not to trust him and not to listen to what he had to say as I was certain that my two brothers had taken my father's side when I had made the allegations of abuse. My mother then told me that she had spoken to my brother and that he was downstairs and wanted to speak with me. I decided to drop down and have a chat with him. As we spoke, my brother told me that my father was staying in a B&B while out on bail and that his health was not good. I realised that my brother's only interest was in my father's welfare and that he had no interest in my life. When he asked me if I had any concept of what the trial was doing to my father, I told him that I didn't care and that I was more interested in building a life for myself. I told him in no uncertain terms that my father had raped me and that he should be offering his support to me and not to our sick father. Shortly afterwards, I told my brother that I was heading off to bed for the night as I had a heavy day ahead of me. The following morning, as I lay in bed, I wondered how the day would pan out. I was very nervous about taking the stand. As I lay in bed, I heard a knock on my hotel room door. It was my mother. She asked me to hurry as we were apparently late for the court case. I got out of bed and dressed quickly. Twenty minutes later, I walked into the courtroom, with my mother and two sisters. The court room was packed. I walked over to my barrister and sat down. Shortly afterwards, the judge spoke to my barrister. My barrister then stood and called me to the witness stand. I felt the shivers as I approached the stand. My barrister realised I was nervous and his initial questions were quite unintrusive. I told the courtroom my name and where I currently lived. Thereafter he asked me to tell the court where I originally came from and what year I moved from there. As I sat in the witness stand, and looked around the room at the jury, members of my immediate family and my father, I began to realise (although I probably always knew) that there would be no winners in this case. As I sat in the witness stand, my barrister began to ask more intrusive questions. I answered as best I could. My barrister made me feel as comfortable as he possibly could while I sat in the witness box. I wasn't sure what to expect as I had never been in a courtroom before in my life. I spent a lot of time telling my story in the witness box as I had to refresh my memory on certain painful instances of abuse. As I started to relate the more sordid elements of my abuse, the courtroom fell quiet. As my barrister continued to ask questions, I continued to provide as much information as I possibly could. I was delighted when the judge interrupted and told the court that we were breaking for an hour for lunch. The woman from the Victim Support Group asked me if I would like to have lunch with her. I immediately accepted. We spent the following hour in the Smithfield area of Dublin where the woman from the VSG told me about the history of the area. It was time to return to the courts and continue from where I had stopped. I walked into the courtroom and spotted my aunt sneering at me. I walked up to my barrister and asked him if it was possible to have her removed from the courtroom. He told me to continue with my testimony and to ignore her. I returned to the witness stand and continued detailing the instances of abuse. I noticed whenever I referred to a serious incident, my aunt coughed loudly to try and distract me. As I continued with my testimony, details of locations of where my father had taken me and raped me streamed into my consciousness. It was like reliving the abuse all over again. I remembered the exact locations where I had been raped. Initially, I explained to the courtroom when the abuse had began. I told them it was when I was about 8 or 9 years old, but that I couldn't be exact on a date. I came across very honest and accurate in my statement to the courtroom. I didn't embellish anything. I also told the courtroom that I wasn't sitting in the witness box to seek revenge on my father and that I was there to show him what he did was wrong. I looked across at my father who was sitting a few yards away from me. I saw teardrops coming from his eyes. I told the court that my father was a cruel person and at the time that he wasn't aware of how cruel he was and the reason that I was sitting there was to tell him in front of the court how difficult it was to survive around him as an infant and a teenager. I also explained to the courtroom how he set one person against the other in our home. He easily managed to manipulate my brothers. My sisters weren't as gullible. I told the court that he never wanted to see any man approaching our house in order to see my sisters or I. I told the court about my father's possessive behaviour when boys from the locality were around chatting to me. He would tell me that he knew what they were thinking about. He thought just because he had a sick mind that everybody else would think the same. He cut conversations short with a boy from the neighbourhood who was a couple of years older than me. My father said that the boy spent too much time staring at me whilst chatting to my father. I told the court that I felt trapped. I couldn't go for a walk with my sisters without our father following us. It became more embarrassing as I got older. One of my neighbours mentioned that she was no longer interested in coming in to visit us because she was fed up with my father grabbing my knee and making crude comments about me to her. I looked at my father as I recounted the stories and I saw his legs shaking with embarrassment. The silence in the courtroom was comforting. I was tearful most of the time as I was getting flashbacks of what had happened to me over the years .As I went through the horrendous part of the story about the night my father tried to strangle me, I noticed a lot of people crying in the court. My mother had told me not to tell the court that a man came to the car and saved my life in case the jurors thought I was unbalanced. I felt that it was important for me to say it anyway. I didn't want to leave anything out. I told them that the man who had saved my life in the early hours of the morning had walked up from the mountain. I didn't know whether he was a real person or not. I told the court about the threats my father had made against me if he was convicted.

When I had finished giving my testimony, my barrister told the court that everything I had told the courtroom matched the statement that I had previously made to the police. He told them that I was accurate on all details. I left the witness box and walked down to my seat. I noticed that my father had his head down looking at his nails. I looked around me and spotted Tony crying. I realised that this was the first time my entire family had heard the full story. I had previously asked a member of my legal team if it would be possible to have my family members removed from the courtroom as I felt details of my abuse might be too painful for them to hear. One of the legal team told me to leave them in there, that they should hear the whole story.

At the time, my two sisters were under 18 years of age and were given the option to give evidence in camera or to the courtroom directly about how my father had treated me. They decided to take the witness stand and tell the courtroom how my father had treated me. My father was stunned as he watched my younger sister approaching the witness box. As my father cleared the sweat from his forehead, he looked at me in a hateful manner. My youngest sister, Aoife, told the courtroom about the things that my father used to tell her about me. She told the courtroom that our father had told her never to believe a word out of my mouth as I was a confounded liar. She thought it was very strange that our father never stopped telling my siblings what a bad person I was. She then recalled an incident where she heard our father threatening me. She said that she had been in her bedroom when she heard screaming coming from the downstairs kitchen. She recognised the two voices. She told the courtroom that she heard my father making threats against me but that at the time she had no idea why he should be making such threats. As she concluded her testimony, my barrister thanked her.

My other sister, Grainne, was then called to the witness stand. As she sat in the witness box, my father blushed and again gave me a dirty look. Grainne told the courtroom that my father constantly told her never to believe a word I said. She also said that he told our neighbours never to believe a word out of my mouth as I was apparently worse than his sisters for telling stories. She then told the court she remembered how our father called her aside on occasion and asked her what sort of conversations I had with her when we went for long walks. She told him that I spent my time talking about school and music. She told the courtroom that she felt very uncomfortable when our father asked her such questions. As my sister continued with her testimony, I looked down at my finger. It had swelled up and was quite painful. I looked across at the representative of the victim support group and told her that my finger had swollen and was hurting me. Shortly after, my sister finished with her testimony and stepped down from the witness stand.

The Judge then asked where my younger brother was. My younger brother had made a statement to the police but had long since left Ireland. The judge ordered that my younger brother would have to be in court to give evidence. The woman from the Victim Support Group asked me if I would like to go to the hospital to have my finger examined. I nodded. As I stood up, I spotted Tony sitting at the back of the courtroom. As soon as we left the Four Courts, the woman from the Victim Support Group drove me to the Mater Hospital to have my finger examined. When we arrived at the Mater, we were obliged to wait there for 2 hours before I was treated. When I left the hospital that night with a bandage on my finger, I returned directly to the hotel where my family and I were staying. As the woman from the Victim Support Group dropped me off at the hotel for the night, she told me that I would have to be very strong the following day during my cross-examination.

The following morning my family and I arrived at the Four Courts early. As soon as we entered the courtroom, we took our seats. Shortly afterwards, the Judge arrived. As soon as the Judge had taken his seat, he asked if the police had managed to contact my younger brother. A policewoman approached the Judge's stand and told the Judge that they were still trying to contact my younger brother. Shortly afterwards, the Judge adjourned the case for the remainder of the day. When I returned to my hotel, a police officer told me that although they had now managed to contact my younger brother, they were having difficulties persuading him to return to Ireland to give testimony. I was livid. I had travelled back from America where I had managed to create a life for myself and my brother who my father had beaten on umpteen occasions was refusing to return to give evidence. I asked the police officer if he would give me my brother's phone number and that I would personally call him and ask him to travel to Dublin to give evidence. As soon as I returned to my bedroom, I rang my brother. Initially, he refused to speak to me and hung up. When I rang again, he complained about how the Irish police were treating him. He told me that they had threatened to jail him if he refused to return. He said that he had no interest in returning to Ireland and that the case would have to continue in his absence. I told him the policewoman had suggested that the case could be struck out if he didn't return to give evidence. I then told him that if he wouldn't come willingly that the police could apply to have him extradited, like they do in the United States. I told him that I would much prefer it if he would come of his own accord. As I continued to discuss the matter with my brother, my mother and two sisters entered my room. Slowly, his mood began to change. I told him that if he failed to return to give evidence that I would never speak to him again as long as I lived. I could hear him crying on the other end of the phone. Seconds later, my brother consented to return. I spent a while having a friendly conversation with him afterwards. As soon as I hung up the phone, my mother and sisters rushed downstairs and told the police that I had managed to persuade him to come over. The police sergeant arrived in my room moments later and thanked me. He asked me if I knew what flight my brother had arranged. I told him that my brother had said that he would ring back as soon as he had arranged a flight. Moments later, the phone rang. It was my brother. He said that he was having difficulty arranging a flight. The police officer told me to tell him that they would arrange his flights and that I could ring him later on and give him the details. I thanked my brother and told him that I would see him in court the following day. Later that evening, my eldest brother arrived at the hotel. He was very surprised to hear that our younger brother would be travelling over from England to give evidence the following day. The next morning, I stood in the main hallway of the Four Courts with my mother and the counsellor from the Galway Rape Crisis Centre waiting for my younger brother to arrive. My two sisters remained outside. As soon as the taxi that was carrying my younger brother arrived outside the courts, my two sisters ran back in and told us that he had arrived. I spotted Tony chatting to my younger brother as they entered the Four Courts. They then walked over and began speaking to my mother. Niall gave me a hug. As my brothers spoke to my mother, I began to realise that although they sympathised with me, they also sympathised with my father. I realised from the tone of their conversation that they both wished that I had never pressed charges against my father. We then walked into the courtroom and sat down. Niall sat beside the woman from the Galway Rape Crisis Centre. My father looked at my younger brother quizzically. As the Judge began to address the court, I found it difficult to concentrate.

My mother was then called to give evidence. My mother told the barrister that my father was a manipulative individual who had managed to get his own way on a constant basis. She also told the barrister that my father constantly lied. The barrister asked my mother many questions. She managed to answer the majority of his questions. Tony sat beside my father's sister, directly behind me. My father's sister sneered when my mother was cross-examined. When my mother stepped down from the witness box, my father laughed at her and leaned down to say something to the interpreter. I'm sure whatever he said wasn't nice. The judge then asked if my younger brother was in court. A police officer informed the court that he was in the courtroom. Shortly afterwards, the Judge adjourned the case until the following day.

Later that evening, my mother, two sisters and I had dinner with my two brothers. My brothers told me that they were very worried about taking the stand and that they were afraid of what the barristers might ask them. After the dinner, I returned to my hotel with my mother and two sisters and went to bed.

The following day in court, there was an unexpected turn of events. As my barrister was addressing the courtroom, he inadvertently informed the court that there had been a barring order placed against my father from approaching my mother's dwelling place. My father's barrister jumped to his feet immediately and complained vehemently about the slur on his client's name. He asked what relevance this comment had on the ongoing case and claimed that such a remark could unjustly influence the jury's decision. The Judge dismissed the case for the day. My barrister informed me that there would be a legal argument regarding his remark and that the issue would have to be resolved before the case could continue. Shortly afterwards, I left the courtroom and returned to my hotel. That evening, as I sat in my hotel room watching TV, my mother visited me and informed me that my two brothers wanted to drop up and have a chat with me. When they arrived in my room, Tony spoke to me about the case. My brother then asked me if this was the first or second floor of the Hotel. I was surprised that my brother was unsure of the floor he was on. As he spoke to me, he approached my bedroom window and looked out. I told him that I was on the first floor. Moments later, my two sisters entered my room. When my younger sister heard my eldest brother commenting on the white stairway outside my bedroom, she walked over to the window and viewed it. She then told me that it was nice that I had a white stairway leading up to my window. Shortly afterwards, my mother told my siblings that it was time to leave as I needed a good night's sleep. Moments later, they all left. Shortly after my family had left, the woman from the Galway Rape Crisis Centre knocked on my door. I was happy to see her. She asked me how I felt. I told her that I was nervous but happy that it was nearly over. I went straight to bed as soon as she left.

At 3am, I heard a loud knocking and woke up. I looked at my bedroom door and thought that somebody was knocking on the door. Slowly, I realised that the noise was coming from the other end of the room. I looked at my bedroom window and spotted the outline of a person behind the partially pulled curtains standing in front of the window. I approached the window, believing that I was imagining things. As I pulled back the curtains the remainder of the way, I realised that it was my father standing outside knocking on the window. As soon as he saw me, he began to knock louder. I turned and rushed out of the room as quickly as I could. I rushed down the hall and knocked relentlessly on my mother's bedroom. When she opened the door, I asked her what room my younger brother was staying in. She realised that I was in a state of panic and tried to calm me down. As soon as she told me what room my brother was staying in, I ran as fast as I could to his room. I banged on his door. I told him to hurry up and open his door. I was trembling with fear. When he opened the door, I urged him to dress quickly. He dressed quickly and dialled the reception number from his bedroom. He then tried to phone the police. There was no answer. He then told me to return to my mother's room and that he would drop down to the reception to see if he could phone the police from there. When I returned to my mother's room, I told her what had happened. She told me not to worry that my father was now desperate and would try anything. Moments later, my brother returned and told us that they had looked outside and that if my father had been outside the window that he had now fled. My mother then asked me if I felt strong enough to return to my room alone. I told her that I would be fine. When I returned to my room, I had a very restless night.

The following morning, I was practically asleep entering the courtroom. As I sat in my seat, I prayed to my great grandmother to be with me. As soon as I had sat down, a police officer approached and apologised that I had difficulty contacting the police the previous night. Shortly afterwards, the Judge arrived and everyone in the courtroom stood up. My eldest brother was the first witness called. During my brother's testimony, my barrister asked my brother if he could recall an occasion when he was jogging with me and our father arrived and drove off with me in the car. He confirmed the incident. During my brother's testimony, he confirmed some of the statements that I had made but was on occasion unable to confirm others. Although my brother was hesitant in responding to many of the questions my barrister asked him, I felt that my eldest brother gave honest testimony while he was on the stand.

As soon as my eldest brother was finished on the stand, my younger brother was called. During my younger brother's testimony, my barrister asked him if he could remember watching a pornographic video that my father had supplied. My brother denied ever having watched such a video. My barrister then asked my brother if I had ever been left alone with my father to the best of his recollection. My brother responded that I had never been left alone with my father and that the three of us; my eldest brother, my younger brother and I were always together. My younger brother's testimony in general was not supportive of my case. When my younger brother finished giving his testimony, I noticed that my mother was upset with the comments he had made in the witness box. Moments later, the Judge adjourned the case to the following day.

As we walked out of the courtroom, Tony walked beside our father and my father's sister. My mother, livid at this stage, shouted at my eldest brother, "Thank you very much… You weren't a bit supportive of Barbara…it looks like you enjoyed what happened to her… I will never see you again as my son over what you've done…You purposely failed to answer some of the questions you were asked." My mother began to shout and told him that he was a disgrace for siding with my father.

My father's legal team were stunned as they walked directly into a slagging match between my mother and eldest brother. My father and his sister merely walked past my mother and didn't engage in the ongoing row. As the row continued, I grabbed my mother's arm and told her that my brother had in fact told the truth to the best of his ability. I told her that my younger brother's testimony was hostile and that if she wanted to accuse anyone of letting me down that she should direct her comments and ire at him. My mother looked at me and gradually calmed down. Tony walked over to me and said "I didn't protect my father". I told him that he had been honest in the witness stand and that I had no problem with his testimony. My mother and I then returned to the hotel.

Later that evening, as I sat in the lounge of the hotel where I was staying, my two brothers arrived and joined our company. As soon as I spotted them approaching, I stood up and told my mother I was heading to my room. Before I could leave, my brothers arrived at the table and asked all of us if we would like a drink. I told my younger brother that I had no intention of remaining in his company. My younger brother merely sneered as he sipped his hot whiskey and said, "'As a matter of fact, Dad's solicitor told us today that you are stupid and that you came across in the witness like a thick eejit.....he also said that you are a bad liar and that you didn't make sense when you were in the witness box." My mother, two sisters and elder brother merely sat there and allowed my brother to continue in this vein. He then told me that my father was going to kill me for making the allegations that I had made in court. He informed me that my father's lawyer told him that my father's sentence would be lenient if he was found guilty. As my brother continued making these hurtful remarks, I asked my sisters and mother how they could endure the present company that had taken their father's side. My mother and sisters merely looked blankly at me. Tony then commented that I had been very fortunate that the case had not been thrown out of court as my mother had accosted him outside the courts. Before I left, I turned to Niall and asked him why he hadn't the guts to stand up to our father who had beaten him as a young boy. For a moment, he was lost for words. I then told him that at least I had the guts to stand up against my father for what he had done to me. My brother merely stood there speechless. I then returned to my room and cried. I realised that my younger brother totally supported my father. Later that evening, my mother and two sisters arrived in my room. Immediately, they began chastising me for the comments I had made to my younger brother. When they left my room shortly afterwards, I felt very alone. An hour later, the woman from the Galway Rape Crisis Centre dropped in for a chat. I told her what had transpired. She told me not to worry and that she would have a word with my mother. Later that evening, my sisters returned to my bedroom and remonstrated with me over comments my counsellor had made to my mother about jeopardising the case.

The following day, I was recalled to the witness stand where my father's barrister began to cross-examine me. At first, he showed me a drawing of my original home in Kinnvarra and asked me several questions about the house and the walls of the house. He then asked me if the walls had been made out of concrete. I replied that I believed the walls were made out of concrete. He then asked about the location of the different bedrooms in the house and where my bedroom was located in relation to my parents' room. As his questions continued, I described the various rooms in the house and where they were located in relation to one and other. When I had finished my description, the barrister told me that the map he had was at variance to what I had described. I replied that the map the barrister had was probably quite dated and that my father had built a wall in the sitting room and had made several structural changes to the house over the past few years. The barrister then asked me about the statement I had made to the police and the testimony that I had given in court regarding the locations where my father had raped me. He asked me how I could be so accurate about dates and locations as some of these incidents had happened very late at night. Before I could respond, he handed me a photograph with a picture of an old gate on it and asked me if I recognised it and if I could identify where the gate was located. I immediately identified the location as a place where my father had raped me one night. He then asked how I could be certain of the location as the incident had occurred very late at night. I innocently replied that there were lights on my father's car. The court room erupted in laughter. The judge ordered every one to be silent. I continued and told the court that it was as if I had had an accident at the location and that the location was printed indelibly on my mind. The barrister then asked me if I had a boyfriend when I was 18. I replied that I had friends, but not a boyfriend. I told the barrister that I had found it practically impossible to have a boyfriend at the time as my father was constantly controlling my life. When the barrister asked me another question, I asked him to repeat the question as I had difficulty hearing him. He asked me if I was deaf. I was stunned. I replied that there may have been several things wrong with me due to my experiences, but that I certainly wasn't deaf. Shortly afterwards, the cross-examination finished and I left the witness box. As I approached my seat, I overheard my father's barrister speaking to my father and my father's sister. The barrister advised my father that it would be better if he took the stand. My father's sister asked the barrister if it would benefit my father's case if they were able to produce a psychologist's report indicating my father's apparent ill-health. My father's barrister replied that it would have little or no bearing on the case at this stage. I walked straight past my father and aunt directly out of the court house.

My Father Takes The Witness Stand

When I returned to the courtroom after lunch, my father was called to give evidence. My mother turned to me and said that she was very surprised to see my father taking the stand. The interpreter stood beside my father. My father's barrister first asked my father where he was originally from. My father replied that he was born in England. My father's voice was quite loud and he had no need of the microphone that was positioned on the witness stand. As the barrister continued, my father began answering all the questions in Irish. Moments later, my father's barrister sat down and said that he was finished questioning my father. My barrister then stood up and began questioning my father. Initially, my barrister asked my father several general questions. After a moment, my barrister asked my father to describe the relationship he had with his children. My father nearly choked and angrily asked the barrister "what do you mean, relationship with my children". My barrister replied that he was asking about the general relationship my father had as a parent with his children.

My father calmed down and said that the relationship was "like all normal families have with their children. You know what normal families do.....sit around and watch television." My barrister then asked him if the programmes were in Irish or English? My father answered that he didn't really watch much television and that he had bought the television for the children. My barrister then asked my father what programmes he watched on television. My father replied that he generally only ever watched TNG, the Irish language station. He then asked my father what his other interests were. My father told him that he used to work around the house. My barrister then asked my father if he had any idea why his daughter should be making such allegations and when all the trouble started. My father again misunderstood the question and responded that the trouble began in 1978, the year I was born. My barrister looked at him quizzically and asked him to explain. My father replied that that was the year I was born and that was the year all his problems began. My father began telling his life story and how a member of my mother's family had stabbed him. He then unrolled his sleeve and pointed to the scar on his arm. Slowly, he realised he had made a mistake and that it was the other arm. When he mentioned this to the barrister, the whole courtroom erupted in laughter. My mother looked at me, her hand on her mouth. When my barrister tried to resume with his questioning, my father merely ignored his question and continued retelling the more sorrowful episodes of his life. As my barrister was not a fluent Irish speaker, he had no idea my father was ignoring his questions until the interpreter translated my father's remarks from Irish to English. As my father continued telling "HIS" story, he began to verbalise with his hands. Gradually, his testimony was becoming farcical. My father then recounted the story of when his brother-in-law forced him to buy several bottles of poitin. As the interpreter translated, cries of laughter could be heard around the courtroom. Even the judge had difficulty restraining himself from laughing. Eventually, my barrister asked my father if he could possibly answer the questions he was asked and not spend the day regaling the courtroom with stories. When my father finally finished, my barrister asked him again why his daughter had made such allegations. My father replied, "Her mother put her up to it." The barrister replied "why do you think your wife would want to do this?" Without hesitation my father replied in English "she would do it out of spite". The barrister then lifted a bunch of papers and asked my father what he thought about the statements I had made to the police. My father replied aggressively in Irish, "Malai Breaga (a bag of lies). At this stage, my father began responding to my barrister's questions in English. My father looked directly at my barrister and repeated in English this time, "A bag of lies." My youngest sister, who was sitting beside me, began to laugh. My father heard her laughing and immediately lost control. He also lost track of what he was saying. I noticed that my father had been giving my youngest sister the evil eye. I looked over at my sister when I noticed that my father was staring at her. I smiled at her. I noticed that she had her hands on her mouth trying to stop herself from smirking about my father's comments. She stopped laughing immediately when he kept his eye on her.

The barrister then asked my father what was his English like growing up? My father told him that his English was poor and that they generally only spoke Irish in the locality. My barrister then asked my father what standard of English he thought he had. My father said that he had very little use for English. My barrister then produced a letter and asked my father to read the letter out to the courtroom. As he handed the letter to my father, he asked my father if he recognised the signature at the bottom of the letter. My father faltered for a moment, then quietly replied that it was his own signature. As my father had responded in a very quiet manner, my barrister asked him to repeat his answer to the courtroom so that every body could hear. My father duly did as requested. My barrister then asked my father to read out the letter my father had written to the Director of Public Prosecutions. My father read the letter that had been written in English. When my father finished reading the letter, my barrister said no further questions. Shortly afterwards, the Judge adjourned the case for the weekend and told us to return the following Tuesday morning.

As soon as we returned to the hotel, my mother, two sisters and I gathered our belongings and headed home to Galway on the train for the weekend. When we arrived in Galway city, my mother collected the family car at her uncle's house. As we drove from Galway city to Connemara, a row broke out between my mother and I. She asked me not to mention in court the night that she walked into my bedroom and spotted my father standing over my bed. I asked her why not. Suddenly, she slapped me across the face and told me to do as she asked. My two sisters began screaming, shouting at us to stop arguing. The remainder of the journey to Connemara was made in total silence. As I got out of the car, when we arrived home, my mother hugged me and apologised for hitting me. She said that we were all suffering and that she was sorry that she had lost her temper.

The following morning, I rang a travel agent to try and arrange a flight back to the United States as I was confident the case would be finished within a couple of weeks. I booked a flight to travel three weeks later. Later that afternoon, I received a call from my boyfriend in Boston. He was wondering what I was doing and when I would be returning. I told him that I had some family business to finalise and not to worry as I had booked a flight to travel back to Boston in three weeks time. That evening, one of my old class mates dropped around to the house. We discussed old times and eventually she asked me about my life in America. I told her that I had a job I liked, a man I adored and what I believed to be an excellent future in a country where I could leave my shameful past behind. I then showed her a picture of the man I intended to marry one day. I handed her the picture. She looked at the picture, said that he was ugly and then proceeded to rip up the picture in front of my very eyes. I was dumbfounded and asked her why she had ripped up my picture. She merely looked at me and told me that I could do much better for myself. I said nothing. Shortly afterwards, thankfully she left.

When I awoke the following morning, I heard several voices in the kitchen. My mother was discussing the case with some of our neighbours. In general, the neighbour sympathised with my mother and called my father every name under the sun. Several of the neighbours suggested to my mother that I should "name and shame" my father if he was convicted. I remained in bed until I heard the last of them leaving. When I headed down to the kitchen, my mother and her father were discussing the case. As soon as I entered the kitchen they both rounded on me and demanded that I "name and shame" my father after the case if he was convicted. I was in two minds. I had no desire for any publicity and was hoping to quietly leave the country and head back to Boston as soon as the case was finished. I told my mother how I felt and that I had no desire for revenge, merely closure. My mother's father stood up and told me in no uncertain terms that I wouldn't be welcomed back in the house unless I did what my mother asked. When I looked across the room at my mother, she merely repeated what her father had said.

As I returned to Dublin with my mother and two younger sisters on the train, I felt trapped. The trial had been quite exhausting and had left me drained. I had no desire to name my father publicly, as I felt it would merely attract further negative attention to my case. When the train arrived at Heuston Station, we all jumped into a taxi and headed back to our hotel. That afternoon, my younger brother arrived in the hotel. As soon as he spotted my mother and I in the foyer, he rushed over and told us that my father was planning to take the boat from Dun Laoghaire to Holyhead (in Wales) later that night. My brother told us that our father had had a long conversation with him about heading off to England. My brother told us that our father believed that he could escape to Britain and lie low over there for a few years until the case died down. I immediately rang the police and told them what my brother had told us. They told me not to worry as they would have police officers at the port waiting for my father in case he tried to use the port to escape to England.

When I arrived in court the following morning, I was immediately called to the witness stand. I was obliged to read out a Victim Impact Report to the courtroom. The report contained statements made by a psychiatrist and a counsellor I had attended in Galway. After reading the report, I told the court that I was aware of cases of this nature where people convicted received very lenient custodial sentences. I told the court that I felt such sentences were unfair on the victims. I suggested to the courtroom that if my father was found guilty that he should be sentenced to 18 years, the amount of time I had lost due to his despicable behaviour. I also told the court that I was glad that I had managed to survive to tell my story as my father had tried to murder me. I also told the court that I hoped any judgment would help other victims of such crimes throughout rural Ireland come forward and confront their abusers. As I finished, I heard a phone ringing in the judge's office. The judge turned his head and asked the court clerk to "run in and answer the phone." I left the witness box and returned to my seat. Seconds later, the court clerk returned and told the judge that someone wanted to speak to him on the phone. The judge told the court room that such an incident was very unusual. The judge stood up and headed towards the room where the phone rang. I looked across at the woman from the Victim Support Group. She told me not to be concerned. When the Judge returned to the courtroom, he told the court room that he had received a call from the Junior Minister Robert Molloy's office. The Judge said that such a contact was very unusual and that he had no intention of engaging in a conversation with a Civil Servant or politician regarding a legal case that he was trying. He also said that there was no underhand business taking place in his court room. He then informed the court room that he had received two letters from my father's sister and that he had not opened them. He then called my father's sister's to his stand and asked her to take back the unopened letters. My father's sister blushed, approached the Judge's stand and retrieved her unopened letters. The Judge then adjourned the case until after lunch.

When we returned to court after lunch, the two barristers made their final presentations. The Judge then asked the jury to retire and consider a verdict. We returned to the courtroom at 7 o'clock that evening and the Judge asked the jury if they had reached a decision. The jury informed the Judge that they needed more time. They were sent to a Hotel for the night to discuss the matter further. The following morning, we entered the courtroom and the jury still hadn't reached a verdict. That afternoon, we returned to the courtroom. On this occasion, the jury told the judge that they had reached a verdict. Patrick Naughton, my father, had been found guilty. My father nearly collapsed as the verdict was announced. Several people surrounded and congratulated me. Shortly afterwards, the Judge announced sentence on my father. He was sentenced to 11 years imprisonment. My father's demeanour changed. He slumped in his chair. Moments later, two police officers lead my father from the court room. As he passed my mother and I, he began cursing at my mother in Irish and vowed to have his revenge. This incident convinced me to "name and shame my father." He had shown no remorse and was more interested in threatening my mother than apologising to me. As we exited the Four Courts, several journalists approached and asked me questions about the Junior Minister's involvement.

I told them I had no comment on that subject. As I followed the prison officers who were escorting my father out of the courts, I spotted a man who worked for the Irish language station in our locality sitting on a bench with his wife. When my father spotted the man, he stopped and stared at the man with pure hatred in his eyes. The police officers then led my father away to begin his sentence. The case began in October 2001 and finished at the beginning of April, 2002. Mr. Molloy apologised publicly for his behaviour before he resigned, but sadly, I never received a personal apology from Mr Molloy.

FINDING YOURSELF

I stared at the clouds until they became darker,
My bright blue eyes winked at the moon,
Sat like a Buddha on top of the rock
By the sea
Learning how peaceful and calm the sea was,
Dawn came, I sat there in stillness.
Realising the world has the answers,
Just tune in to listen to the wave
Dawn came, I still sat there
Listening to my inner-self.
Listening to the birds singing,
Staring, knowing the world is a beauty.
Realising it's the world that didn't cause pain
Just the people.

REFLECTIONS

As a rule, I prefer not to discuss details of my abuse as I find the subject matter morose. When I attended a drop-in centre in Dublin that provided support to victims of institutional abuse (sadly this was the best the state could offer me) I was constantly reminded of the negativity that surrounds the subject matter of abuse. The poor souls in this centre were constantly comparing the level of abuse they had suffered. It was like a competition to establish who had suffered the most. It became apparent to me at an early stage, that such a centre had little chance of rehabilitating victims of such experiences. With the life experience I have had with people and especially my immediate family, I now find it very difficult to trust. The person I should have been able to trust implicitly, my father, ended up being the person who caused me the most pain.

I have fond memories of relationships that I had in my own hometown in Galway. I had nice men around me that would drive miles to my home to collect me and treat me like a lady. I never gave time to a man who didn't treat me with respect. I became aware that I had a tendency to gravitate towards individuals with acute personality addictions such as alcoholism or gambling. I noticed that people I have met who have endured similar experiences to my own tend to attract (or be attracted) to partners who seem to exhibit similar characteristics to their abuser. They must realise there has to be a time when they need peace in their lives. Over a period of time, I began to realise that I was getting into relationships for the sake of not being alone. I sensed that I needed to be alone for a period of time to heal.

I am a very spiritual person. I firmly believe that it is essential for people to have a positive outlook on life and to embrace all new experiences with an open mind. During my ordeal as a child, I found it very difficult and embarrassing to either come forward and confide in anybody about what was happening to me or to confront my father about his behaviour. Also, as it was my biological father who was abusing me, confronting the issue in my own mind was and still is not an easy matter. Hailing from a rural Catholic community in the West of Galway, the topic of sexual abuse was taboo. Fortunately, during those difficult times, I had the determination never to surrender to the evil that was pervading my life. I have managed to bring in new energy and a new consciousness that ensures that I have my feet in a new life. It hasn't been easy straddling these two Energies within. Furthermore, I found the experience of Shamanic Healing/ Soul Retrieval amazing. It made me so much stronger in myself and at a point where my family can never undermine my self-confidence again. After my father's trial and conviction, I was obliged to reconsider my life and proactively seek a path that would enable my body and soul to heal. Due to my ordeal, my memory lapses at times. I find it very difficult to trust people due to my experiences. When I first thought about writing a book about my experiences, I knew the whole process would be a very difficult and an emotional rollercoaster for me. I was obliged to relive and re-engage with memories that I had managed to suppress. I was obliged to consider the actions of a negligent father. I was also obliged to reconsider the actions of my mother who failed to protect me during my childhood from my father's sexual abuse and also the actions of my siblings who failed to provide adequate support to me during and after my father's trial.

On foot of my father's conviction, I applied to The Department of Health and to other agencies of the state to ascertain whether the state would financially assist me in having certain medical procedures to rectify difficulties I was having with my breathing as I felt the state should have provided me with appropriate medical attention subsequent to my father's trial. Whenever meeting an agent of the state, lip service was the order of the day. I also discovered that victims of domestic sexual abuse receive no compensation from the State for their injuries if the wrongdoer is related to the victim and living under the same roof. I have found dealing with the majority of Civil Servants and Politicians I have met, both perplexing and infuriating. Simply, the State ignored my pleas at every turn. Subsequent to my father's sentencing, Relations with my family soured. Whenever I tried to contact them, I felt they behaved in a condescending manner towards me and treated me as if I was a stranger. After completing a course dealing with all aspects of healing, I decided to enrol in a legal course, which I subsequently completed successfully. My other interests are singing and film. I have recently completed an evening course in scriptwriting and found it very helpful. In my spare time, I thoroughly enjoy singing and hope to produce a record some day.